Attachment for Teachers

ATTACHMENT AWARE SCHOOLS COLLECTION®

The Attachment Aware School series
- Book 1   The Key Adult in School
- Book 2   The Senior Manager in School
- Book 3   The Key Teacher in School
- Book 4   The Team Pupil in School
- Book 5   The Parent and Carer in School

Attachment for Teachers
Attachment in the Classroom
Better Play
Conversations That Matter
Inside I'm Hurting
Little-Mouse Finds a Safe Place
Making Friends
Overcoming Barriers to Learning
School as a Secure Base
Settling to Learn
Teaching the Unteachable
Teenagers and Attachment
Temper Temper!
What About Me?
What Can I Do With The Kid Who…?
You think I'm Evil

Attachment for Teachers

The essential guide for trainee teachers and NQTs

Building confidence and skills for working with the challenging effects of attachment difficulties on behaviour and learning

Marie Delaney

Worth Publishing

worthpublishing.com

First published 2017 by Worth Publishing Ltd
worthpublishing.com

Reprinted 2018

© Worth Publishing Ltd 2017

All rights reserved. No part of this publication may be reproduced, stored in a retrieval system or transmitted in any form, or by any means, electronic, mechanical, photocopying, recording or otherwise, without the prior permission of the publishers, nor be otherwise circulated without the publisher's consent in any form of binding or cover other than that in which it is published and without a similar condition being imposed on the subsequent purchaser.

Printed and bound by CPI Group (UK) Ltd, Croydon, CR0 4YY

British Library Cataloguing in Publication Data
A catalogue record for this book is available from the British Library

ISBN   9781903269374

Cover and text design by Anna Murphy

To Olly - my best friend and supporter

Acknowledgements

As usual I would like to acknowledge the many children and young people with whom I have worked over the last 20 years. They have shown true resilience, perseverance and humour in their darkest moments. It is from them that I have learned the most. They are not mentioned here by name but they are, as always, the main inspiration for this book.

Ideas do not exist in isolation. Thanks to all my tutors and colleagues at Caspari for their knowledge and insights which have helped inform the therapeutic principles in this book. The ideas in *Attachment for Teachers* came out of collaboration and discussion with many great colleagues and friends over the years. It is impossible to name everyone here but I hope they know who they are. I am in their debt.

And finally, to the teachers I have worked with and trained over the years who work tirelessly to improve the outcomes for children in difficult environments and who never give up on the most challenging pupils. They remind us all why we need to keep investing in teacher support and development.

My thanks to my family, for their continuing love, belief in me and unwavering support: to Olly, as always, for his love and unconditional support: to Andrea Perry for her superb editing: and Martin Wood at Worth Publishing for recognising the potential writer in me and his complete commitment to our projects.

Biography

Marie Delaney is a teacher, educational psychotherapist, trainer and writer. She is Director of the Learning Harbour in Ireland. She has extensive experience of working with students who have been affected by traumatic early years experiences and who display challenging behaviour, having worked in non-formal education, mainstream and special school settings. Her main interests are applying therapeutic thinking approaches to understanding learning and behaviour in school, supporting wellbeing of staff and pupils, unlocking learning blocks and developing inclusive approaches. She has trained teachers in several countries and now offers consultancy, training and workshops across the education, social service and youth justice sectors. She is the author of *Teaching the Unteachable* (2008), *What Can I Do With the Kid Who … ?* (2010) Worth Publishing and *Into the Classroom: SEN* (2016) OUP. She is co-author of the British Council's course for teachers on SEN and co-author of the British Council's *Language for Resilience* Report (2016).

Contents

1	Introduction	1
2	Tips to retain your sanity	9
3	Attachment for teachers - an overview	21
4	Challenging behaviours - meet the pupils	57
5	Difficult times	85
6	Some specific difficulties with learning	91
7	The importance of teacher language	111
8	The curriculum as a vehicle - challenges and opportunities	131
9	Managing your wellbeing	141

(continues ...)

Appendix A   **154**
    Observation: an attachment-based pupil profile

Appendix B
    Attachment checklists   **156**

Appendix C   **162**
    CPD (1) - Developing your skills

Appendix D   **166**
    CPD (2) - Applying your learning: case studies

References and weblinks   **179**

Index   **182**

Chapter 1

Introduction

I'm struggling with some of the students in my class who don't seem to respond to the Behaviour Management techniques and approaches I am learning on my PGCE. They seem so emotionally volatile and not ready to learn. I sometimes feel hopeless and don't know what to do with them.
Jamie, trainee secondary teacher

As an NQT or trainee teacher, do you recognise the difficulties that Jamie is having with some of the students in his class? Do you have students or pupils who at times seem unreachable and unteachable? You're not alone.

At times, even the most experienced teachers have pupils in their classes who they find impossible to teach. These pupils take up a lot of our thinking time and energy. They stay in our minds when we go home. We can become frustrated, upset and even de-motivated when they don't seem to want to do any learning, and they disrupt the learning of others in the class. Sometimes our best teaching strategies just don't seem to work with them.

When I initially encountered this kind of pupil in my own classroom, I despaired of finding a way to engage them in learning. And in desperation, I looked around for a different way of thinking, another way to try to understand the nature of the challenges they present, and a new 'lens' for viewing their behaviour. For me, that 'lens' came from the field of educational psychotherapy and in particular Attachment

Theory, which refers to the need all children have, from the beginning of life, for a nurturing, safe relationship with a caregiver. And that need doesn't leave them when they come into school.

What I came to realise was that many of these 'unteachable' pupils will have had poor experiences of relationships with adults in their early life. They may have experienced loss, trauma, abuse and neglect. They may have experienced parents/caregivers who were frightening, inconsistent or emotionally unavailable. They may have learned that adults cannot be trusted to take care of them. And they are often the children and young people most at risk of exclusion, disengagement and dropping out of the education system if we, the adults in school, can't help them.

Pupils with this kind of experience of loss, neglect and trauma in their early years find it hard to cope and succeed in school. They find it hard to settle to learn. They are children and young people who come into school most days with their minds preoccupied by anxieties, fears and worries. For some, school may be the only place which is predictable and safe. Some may still be living in difficult environments; some may now seem to be living in more stable environments such as with loving foster carers, but the impact of their early years will still linger.

THAT SOUNDS DAUNTING …

You might now be feeling daunted by the idea of dealing with the impact of such trauma on pupils in your class. You might be thinking, '*That's all well and good, but I am not a social worker or therapist, I am a teacher*'. And you're right: you are a teacher, and you don't need to change profession. This book is written to help you feel more secure in your teaching and have a far greater range of options available to you than simple behaviour management, so that you can help more pupils to engage in learning.

Nor am I suggesting that you need to know every child's personal history in detail, or develop a different teaching plan for every individual. But this book can help you understand what a particular behaviour (especially challenging behaviour) might be telling you about a pupil's world, about their experience of adults and of learning. This will enable you to understand their needs better, and plan to meet these needs with practical teaching strategies.

Sometimes it will be a matter of doing a small thing to show a pupil you remember them: or maybe simply a case of not reacting in the expected way. Sometimes it will be a matter of knowing how to repair a situation which has gone wrong - no-one gets it right all the time with these pupils. But it's possible to give them a different experience of adult behaviour, and show them that they too can become learners.

Above all, your job is not to fix the problems in a child's life but to create a safe haven in your class for them to experience care, trust and learning. If you connect with these pupils and improve the learning experience, it will have a huge impact on your own experience of teaching, as well as on them.

WHY THIS IS IMPORTANT

> If kids come to us from strong, healthy functioning families, it makes our job easier. If they do not come to us from strong, healthy functioning families it makes our job more important.
>
> Barbara Coloroso kidsareworthit.com

As the quote above from Coloroso suggests, the latter group of pupils are often the ones most in need of our teaching and attention, so it's vital that we spend some time trying to understand them. However, it's also important for us as teachers to find better ways to deal with them, since they are so often the cause of a great deal of our stress and frustration.

Poor pupil behaviour has long been recognised as the main factor in creating teacher stress. As long ago as 1985, Galloway stated: *'Children's behaviour and educational progress are the most important sources of stress in day-to-day classroom events'* and that *'Teacher-child interaction is the most central and enduring source of stress to most teachers'*.

So time spent thinking about these pupils won't be time wasted for you or them. I hope this book will help you to understand and manage these potentially stressful interactions much better, and allow you to keep your own confidence intact, or even increase it. There are ways of working with these children which can mean you could have a lasting positive impact on their lives and which should make your life a bit easier. And keep you in the teaching profession!

WHO ARE THESE PUPILS?

We usually recognise these pupils through their behavioural difficulties and/or their learning difficulties which will often be evident on a daily basis and across a range of classes. We'll usually see their difficulties mostly as *problems with relationships* and *blocks to learning*, which don't seem to be related to cognitive ability.

Behavioural difficulties

- Calling out
- Distracting others
- Arguing and getting angry, often inexplicably
- Lying and stealing
- Rubbishing their own work, ripping it up
- Not being able to accept praise
- Having volatile mood swings
- Ignoring or not following instructions
- Refusing to write or start work
- Running away or out of class
- Bullying others

- Seeming to deliberately provoke the teacher and/or the other pupils
- Wandering, walking around, looking into rooms and cupboards
- Reacting very badly to any changes in the school day or lesson
- Noticing everything about the teacher and not the content of the lesson
- Acting very withdrawn and hard to reach
- Inexplicable reactions e.g. crying and getting very upset at seemingly small things

- Hiding under tables, under stairs
- Finding it difficult to make and maintain friendships
- Laughing at inappropriate moments
- Constantly seeking out attention, even negative attention
- Having issues around food e.g. continually eating, hiding it, stealing it
- Not knowing when to stop joking and messing around, even when others have realised and stopped
- Finding it hard to regulate emotions, even positive feelings, happiness becomes uncontrollable giddiness

Difficulties with learning

- Seeming unable to remember and follow instructions
- Forgetting where they should be, or to bring equipment
- Forgetting or seeming not to understand something they have just read
- Showing a poor sense of cause and effect
- Seeming helpless, unable to do work independently

- Giving up very easily and generally having a sense of hopelessness
- Taking a long time over homework and never getting it finished
- Being unable to focus and pay attention on a piece of work for long
- Needing a lot of 1-2-1 help and support to complete a piece of work
- Not being able to ask for help or attract the teacher's attention appropriately

HOW THESE PUPILS CAN MAKE TEACHERS FEEL

As a teacher, you may often have very strong, difficult-to-manage feelings when dealing with these children and young people. With some you may feel frustrated, helpless, hopeless, incompetent, angry, or manipulated, or you may find yourself always disagreeing with colleagues on how best to teach them. With others, you may feel tired, like nothing is ever enough, rejected, or ignored. You will experience a rollercoaster of powerful, volatile emotions, which can be exhausting and demoralising.

Rest assured, this is *normal* when working with vulnerable, needy children and young people, because you are managing important relationships all day. It is inevitable that your feelings will be engaged.

It can be helpful to understand that a huge percentage of this behaviour *is not meant for you*. It might seem personal and hurtful at times, but it is often a case of pupils re-enacting and re-playing patterns of relationships from their past and present environment. Much of this behaviour is activated by anxiety and lack of trust in the school environment and the adults there, or indeed any adults. Your feelings might also be the result of some more complex psychological processes and unconscious defences which go on every day between teachers and pupils. Understanding these can also make teaching feel easier and more energising (*and see* Chapter 2 *for more on this*). I know that I wish I had learned about all this when I first started teaching: it would certainly have helped me on those days when I went home so fed up that I would spend the evening looking for other jobs!

USING THIS BOOK

Most chapters of this book contain two sections - the theory, and the teaching strategies. As a busy teacher, you probably just want to know what to do about your pupils. You might want to skip the sections on theory and turn to the 'what to do' sections. It is of course your choice. But I would urge you at some point to take the time to look at the theory in each section, in which I explain why certain strategies might work with a certain pupil. The theory is presented in a short, practical format, with the key points revisited from a number of angles, and it offers a framework to help you reflect in a different way on the behaviour of your pupils.

So in this book I'll be encouraging you to look at:

▷ The specific behaviours of a pupil in the classroom learning situation

▷ The feelings evoked, and words used about and around this pupil by staff

▷ What the information you're piecing together might be telling you about the pupil: in particular, answering the following questions,

- ▶ what unmet needs from his or her earlier years is this pupil trying to fulfill through this behaviour?

- ▶ what has this pupil *not* had experience of?

- ▶ what is it that this pupil cannot believe about the teacher and the classroom?

- ▶ what possible teaching strategies might help to meet these needs?

Chapter 2

Tips to retain your sanity

I will explain Attachment Theory in detail in Chapter 3, but before launching into that, you might find it reassuring to know that there are some key principles which can be applied by all teachers without a detailed knowledge of the theory. In other words, there are some teaching tips which will help you to remain sane in the midst of the day-to-day classroom challenges we all get presented with. Above all, pupils with attachment difficulties require us to cultivate a certain way of thinking about the classroom, relationships and learning. It can seem overwhelming to begin by thinking about the specifics of individual pupil difficulties, so it might help to remember these 9 'Golden Principles' in your busy teaching day.

In fact of course these tips won't only help children and young people with attachment difficulties, but should help all the pupils in your class: and last, but no means least, you.

1   Manage your own emotional state and wellbeing

Teaching can be physically and emotionally exhausting. It's not surprising that so many teachers become ill in the school holidays. We are often working on adrenaline, with little fuel left in the tank by the end of term. Getting ill is the body's way of letting us know we have been overdoing things and not looking after ourselves. It's vital to pay attention to your own wellbeing, both mental and physical. So be aware of your feelings, learn to recognise when you're not coping, and don't be afraid to ask for help. Asking for, accepting or being offered help really isn't a sign of incompetence. Even the most experienced teachers struggle with certain pupils at times.

It's also important to remember that *our* emotional state and reactions to behaviour as teachers have the biggest impact on *pupil* emotions and behaviour. Pupils come into school every day and more or less do the same thing - sometimes a bit better, sometimes a bit worse - and what makes the biggest difference to them is *the reaction of the adults around them*. Remember also that the only person you really have control over is yourself - control over how you react and how you manage your feelings. On a bad day some pupils will challenge you to the extreme and there will be times when you feel incompetent and unsure what to do. Make sure you are in the best shape to deal with this kind of feeling. Accept that feelings matter in teaching and learning, and be prepared to -

- **acknowledge what you *feel***
- ***think* about where it might be coming from**
- **and *do* something about it**

Some of the feelings might be related to your situation and come from you, feelings you bring with you from outside school, for example. But some of your feelings might be coming from the vulnerable, anxious children or young people you are teaching, and might be giving you a good indication of how they are really feeling. This is an example of **projection** (*see* Box 1).

Whatever the feelings, they need to be managed as well as your physical wellbeing. Don't feel guilty about paying attention to looking after yourself.

BOX 1 PROJECTION

When we have unbearable, painful feelings, we may unconsciously externalise them, 'pushing them out' and trying to attribute them to others. We can't bear to think about them and so we 'look' - unconsciously - for another person to 'hold' them, to have them and take them away from us. It's a process which begins with babies and toddlers when they feel overwhelmed by unknown and unmanageable feelings and project them out onto someone else, usually the mother, for that person to make sense of. We can learn to bear such feelings if a caring adult helps us to understand and manage them. Eventually we learn to do it largely for ourselves.

But this isn't something which happens only with troubled children and young people. It's something that happens to all of us in our daily life, when we try to manage extremely difficult and painful feelings. What any of us need at such times is a calm, containing adult to empathise, reflect and respond appropriately to us. Unfortunately, children with attachment difficulties often haven't had such a person to reliably do that for them, and have had to struggle with these feelings on their own.

How you are feeling when you're with a pupil may give you an indication of what they are feeling. The task is to recognise which feelings are your own, and which may be being projected. When you can work this out, then it becomes easier to be that calm, containing adult who can show your pupil a way to manage their difficult feelings.

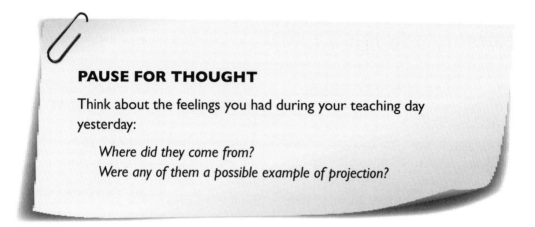

PAUSE FOR THOUGHT

Think about the feelings you had during your teaching day yesterday:

Where did they come from?
Were any of them a possible example of projection?

2 Allow yourself to not know all the answers

You don't need to be perfect. Give up the idea that you need to know everything and have to come up with immediate and appropriate responses to every problem behaviour or learning difficulty. That will never be possible. Allow yourself instead to *be curious* about what's happening with the children and young people presenting challenges, and give yourself permission to not know all the answers.

As teachers, we think that we need to know the answers to and meaning of everything that happens in our classes. And we work in systems which reinforce this idea. However, in order to work effectively with children with very troubled backgrounds and attachment difficulties it's more important to adopt an approach of curiosity and to let go of the idea that you will always immediately know how to react to a situation. Often it's a case of noticing and commenting on what is happening, and wondering about it, rather than rushing to fix it. So we need to practise noticing what is happening without judging it or trying to come up with an immediate solution. Not easy!

This way of working tries to move away from a *reactive*, problem-focused way of looking at behaviour and towards a more *reflective*, exploratory way of responding. Build in pauses for thinking - for you and for your pupils - so that you can *reflect* rather than be continually firefighting and reacting.

Letting go of perfectionism will allow you to be a compassionate human being who is allowed to make mistakes while learning what works best with individual students. Of course we all want to do our best and be as good as possible in our jobs. However, the continual pressure to be excellent and to be perfect sets teachers up for stress and burnout. There is an inevitable trial-and-error approach needed to dealing with challenging behaviour and attachment difficulties. An attitude of *being curious and learning from what is happening* is more important than perfectionism and 'knowing' what to do all the time.

Contrasting approaches

(Developed from origial work by Mia Beaumont)

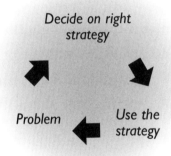

Problem-focused approach

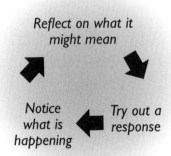

Trial-and-error approach

3 Notice patterns of behaviour, words and feelings

Take a step back from your reactions to a behaviour and try to notice *patterns* in what happens with the behaviour around a pupil. Noticing patterns means noticing the *feelings* evoked in the adults, the words used by the adults around the child or young person, and the types of *reactions* regularly played out in response to what the pupil is doing. Pattern-spotting involves viewing the interaction and the effects on both parties, on ourselves as the teacher and on the pupil.

So if something happens once in your class it is likely to be random: twice, could be coincidence: but three or more times suggests it is a pattern. Patterns of behaviour can tell you something about a child's need or previous experience of adults. Sometimes these patterns are so strong that you can get caught up in re-enacting relationships from the pupil's own life or your own. This is called **transference** (*see* Box 2). The words used around a child or young person can also give an indication of the pattern they are used to creating. Noticing a pattern is the first step towards breaking a negative interaction, and creating the possibility of something more constructive taking its place.

BOX 2 TRANSFERENCE

The unconscious phenomenon known as transference may be at work, when, for example, feelings and attitudes from a relationship with a child's main carers from the past are 'transferred' and are played out, or re-experienced, in a later relationship with a teacher.

You might find yourself acting out a relationship which is not about you and the pupil but a re-enactment of a relationship from the pupil's life or from your own life. Some examples of this might be:

1 the child who seems to go out of their way to cross the path of a teacher with whom they continually have conflict

2 the child who seems to take an instant dislike to a new teacher, despite the adult's best efforts to engage the pupil.

Transference can be triggered by all kinds of things: for example, a look, a tone of voice, a way of dressing, a role, even a way of walking. It occurs because unconsciously, we are trying to understand someone (usually someone we do not know very well) by making an assumption that they are similar to someone else whom we know. It is a fundamental process which happens to all of us in our attempts to make sense of our relationships with other people, to keep our world a bit more predictable and ourselves safe.

Be aware that this can work the other way round as well. A teacher can find themselves reacting badly to a particular pupil for no apparent reason; the child or young person may be triggering a reminder of the teacher's relationship with, for example, their own child or sibling.

> **PAUSE FOR THOUGHT**
>
> Think of a student you find challenging or difficult to teach.
>
> *Can you recognise any patterns of behaviour and interaction with this pupil?*
>
> *Do you notice any patterns in the way you and your colleagues talk about this pupil?*
>
> *How could you begin to break these patterns?*

4 Think developmentally rather than chronologically

Pay less attention to a pupil's chronological age and consider what stage they seem to be at in *child development terms*. Children with attachment difficulties often exhibit the behaviour and reactions of a child of a younger age and will often revert to this in times of stress. A 14-year-old who hasn't learned how to regulate their emotions may be reacting aggressively to you in the same way that a 2-year-old might have a tantrum in the supermarket. Neither have learned to 'regulate' - *contain and manage* - their extreme emotions or to express their needs appropriately.

Some students won't have had the opportunity to develop the social and emotional skills we expect from others at the same chronological age. Remember that some children's life experiences haven't taught them the necessary skills for learning and behaving appropriately in class: or, in fact, they have been effectively taught the opposite. For example, we often want students to wait their turn before answering in class: some children will have learned that if you wait to be noticed by an adult, you will get nothing or get ignored. So it may sometimes be necessary to ask yourself, '*How would I think about and react to this behaviour if it were that of a younger child?*' (*and see* Chapter 3). Omnipotence is one example (Box 3).

BOX 3 OMNIPOTENCE

Omnipotence is a defence mechanism which comes into play when we feel threatened, powerless or not in control. It can happen when a child feels powerless or has little control over their lives outside school or it can mean that a child has had to be an 'adult' way beyond their years at home.

Such pupils can act in school as if they need to control and know everything. They find it hard to be taught because they can't accept the state of not knowing: it reminds them of their vulnerability. They do not want the teacher to have the power of knowing more than them, which can feel like power over them. Unconsciously, they may believe that if they do not allow the teacher to teach them, they will not have to experience this vulnerability. Staff can get very frustrated at not being able to 'help' or 'teach' them.

By trying to control their environment, the child attempts to prevent catastrophes from happening and from allowing anyone to use power over them. We often see it exhibited by children who are in care and who might feel that adults have control over their lives. The child is in effect often cut off from the world and relationships. They act as if they want to be feared and admired, but underneath are often fearful (see p.74).

IMPLICATIONS FOR THE TEACHER

If this defence of omnipotence is in operation, it may feel as if you are engaging with a battle of wills with a pupil over who is in control of the class. You may find yourself refusing even reasonable requests, and thinking, *'I'm the teacher, not him.'* The pupil will need boundaries from you, and space to feel they have some control of their situation. Try to keep strong, safe boundaries, but give some choice and don't get drawn into fighting unnecessary battles. Of course by changing the way we react to something, we hope that it will create a different interaction with the student, and thus cause an improvement in their behaviour and learning.

> **PAUSE FOR THOUGHT**
>
> Think of a student you find challenging or difficult to teach.
>
> *Does the description of the gap between developmental age and chronological age help you understand his or her behaviour?*
> *What kind of activities/approaches did you or could you use to show understanding of this gap?*
> *Do you notice any patterns in the way you and your colleagues talk about this pupil?*
> *How could you begin to change that pattern?*

5 Try differently, rather than try harder

Stop trying hard in a direction which doesn't work, and be prepared to try doing things differently. When we're struggling, we tend to just work harder and spend even more hours planning our lessons. This can be counter-productive, because we are actually doing more of something which isn't working. We have a tendency in education to keep doing more of the same thing because we think or believe that it should work. So we need to find a different way of thinking.

Don't be afraid to trust your own instincts at times. Sometimes 'experts' and teacher training programmes take away your own common sense. Children with attachment difficulties don't always need adults with great specialist knowledge. They need adults who can get alongside them, listen without judging, comment and wonder aloud about what is going on for them. This is the type of thing which we often do with younger children in a family setting. *Being with* a child is often more important than *doing something* to them. Relationship building is sometimes more important than getting through your lesson plan.

6 Stop trying to control others

As I mentioned earlier - we can't control others, only our own reaction to others. By this I mean that we can try to manage behaviour and learning with good planning and strategies, but ultimately we can only *influence* what happens in the classroom: we cannot totally control other people. We can choose to control our own reactions, ways of relating and ways of thinking. This of course seems obvious when we're not stressed, but with some children and young people it's very easy to get hooked into their pattern of behaving and relating: for example, getting hooked into battles with them which are actually not that important to win.

7 Keep a focus on what is working well

Most discussions around pupils presenting challenging behaviour are crisis- and problem-focused. Meetings are called with parents/carers and other professionals because something is going wrong. But it's really important to also spend time looking at *what is going well*. We need to find out what works for pupils with problems, and do more of that, rather than focusing continually on the problems.

For your own sanity in class, it's useful to remember that good strategies work most of the time, with most pupils. If we are not careful, we can go home thinking only about the bad points of our day. Don't lose sight of what is working with the majority of pupils and keep in mind the positives of your day (*see* p.150). But also allow yourself to think compassionately about those who are struggling, even if they seem to be attacking you at times!

8 Understand the difference between *equality* and *equity*

Equality means everyone getting the same, but equity means everyone getting what they need. If you are worried about giving some pupils a different type of attention, remember that no-one can be 100% fair all of the time and it is more important to make sure everyone is getting what they need. Other students understand this concept, if you are clear about it.

9 Focus on creating safety

Feeling safe is important for all children and young people learning in a classroom, but safety is a particular concern for pupils with attachment difficulties. Children who have learned to trust adults in their early years and who have had an experience of an adult who can take care of them in a nurturing way (*secure attachment, see Chapter 3*) generally learn to trust the teacher to keep the class safe and can cope with some uncertainty. Children who have had less security in their early years, and who have not yet learned to trust adults, often react badly to uncertainty and need constant reassurance about their safety in the classroom, even if they are at time the ones making it unsafe with their behaviour.

You will already know many techniques for classroom management and creating learning environments. Linking these techniques to safety and underlying emotional needs is the bridge to supporting children and young people with attachment difficulties. It is vital to create a supportive, co-operative classroom environment where difference is celebrated and students help each other (*for more on this see* pp.27-31).

PAUSE FOR THOUGHT

Do you agree with these golden principles?
Are there any which you would like to focus on in your next lesson?
Are there any other tips which help you to remain sane?

Chapter 3

Attachment for teachers - an overview

This is a book which focuses on practical ideas and guidance. However, in order to understand the behaviour of pupils who present us with really challenging behaviour, it's necessary to understand the basics of Attachment Theory.

Attachment Theory was originally developed by John Bowlby (1988) who concluded from his research that infants are pre-programmed to seek attachment - proximity, and a close connection - with their primary care giver, usually the mother - for safety and relationship. His work was developed further by Mary Ainsworth (1969), who found four categories of attachment:

- **securely attached**
- **insecure ambivalent-resistant**
- **insecure avoidant**
- **insecure disorganised**

In more recent years connections have been made by education practitioners such as Heather Geddes (2006) and Louise Bombèr (2007, 2011) about the effects of insecure attachment on learning and behaviour in school. Neuroscientists such as Schore (2001) and others have also researched and identified the negative effects on the wiring of the brain of unmitigated exposure to danger, inconsistent care and stress. This evolving body of research sheds light on those pupils who seem unable to settle to learn, the ones who concern us most in class and in school. Those children and young people are likely to have had a less than ideal start to life.

But let's begin by understanding *secure attachment*, and how that affects learning and behaviour in class.

SECURE ATTACHMENT

What is it and what does it look like in class?

A key concept of Attachment Theory is that infants are pre-programmed to develop attachment behaviour to their primary caregiver - usually the mother. *Attachment behaviour* describes the way in which the infant and mother negotiate a way of responding to each other in the early months of a child's life. The aim of this attachment behaviour is for the infant is to gain proximity or contact with the *attachment figure*, and with it the associated feelings of safety and security. If the baby can obtain this proximity and contact, he or she can use this relationship as a '*secure base*' from which to develop and explore the world. The baby seeks attachment, and returns to the secure base when he or she feels alarmed, upset or anxious.

The young child learns about his own feelings by the response they elicit. If he cries when he is hungry and is fed, for example, he learns to expect this response. The mother also uses words to try to name what is or might be going on for her child, and to make sense of his experience for him. When the mother is able to respond in this way, paying attention to the baby's needs, and gives a name to her baby's feelings, the feelings can be 'contained' and are less likely to become overwhelming for the child. *Containment* implies that the mother has recognised, understood, thought about and if appropriate, 'reflected back' her baby's feelings in a manageable way. For example, when a baby cries, the mother may pick him up, suggesting what might be happening: "*I know, you're frightened, that was a very loud noise, wasn't it? You thought I had gone away, but Mummy's here.*"

When the mother's response is fairly consistent, the child learns to trust that this is an adult behaviour he or she can expect. Children with this experience develop internal worlds where there is a representation of an attachment figure, a secure adult, who will not reject or humiliate them when they need understanding.

Separation and learning

The child can thus develop the confidence to 'separate' from the caregiver and develop a sense of self, secure in the knowledge that he is still being thought about and remembered by his caregiver in her absence. He comes to learn that a separation can be tolerated without the world falling apart, as he has a secure memory of this containment and responsive interaction. For learning to take place, separation of mother and child needs to take place, because learning can only occur in the separate space between the child and the adult.

Children learn that they can be a separate human being, with their own thoughts and experiences, and that their caregiver will remember them when they are not in direct contact all the time. For example, the child might be playing on the playmat whilst the mother is doing something else nearby. They learn that they can be 'held in mind' by the adult when they are not with them.

The effects of secure attachment

So securely attached children develop a close attachment to their caregiver and learn to trust that the adults will care for them. But at the same time, they also learn to separate out enough from the adult to get on with things on their own, to trust their own thinking. They will usually have learned to play with others and to play by rules. They can wait their turn and learn to share the attention of the adult. They can also bear the feelings of frustration when something goes wrong, because they have had an experience of an adult being able to manage their overwhelming feelings alongside them. They might still be upset or unhappy at times, but they can manage these feelings or expect an adult to help them through this. They develop basic trust and confidence that others will be helpful when asked. Through their experience of thinking adults, they learn empathy, the ability to understand their own feeings and those of others. This ability to view the world from another person's perspective is vital for children to be able to socialise and learn in a group.

Over time, securely attached babies and young children do better in terms of:

- Self-esteem
- Independence and autonomy
- Resilience in the face of adversity
- Long-term friendships
- Trust, intimacy and affection
- Social coping skills
- Ability to manage impulses and feelings
- Empathy, compassion and conscience
- Relationships with parents, caregivers and other authority figures
- Positive and hopeful belief systems about self, family and society
- Behavioural performance and academic success

(Levy 1998, *cited in* Bombèr 2007)

Securely attached pupils generally cope better in schools because they have the skills needed for learning. We expect them to be capable in the following areas.

> **Capacities of securely attached pupils**
>
> - Staying focused and blocking out distractions
> - Understanding and keeping to rules and boundaries
> - Waiting their turn, sharing the attention of the teacher
> - Asking for and accepting help
> - Bearing the feelings of frustration and disappointment when they get it wrong
> - Having an optimistic attitude to learning and mistakes
> - Feeling safe and taking risks with new learning

If children have had a nurturing, safe environment in their early years, they will have developed many of these skills. They come into school and can usually play independently, take risks, ask for help, wait for and share attention, and relate positively to peers and teachers. They can usually manage when something goes wrong or they make a mistake. They can regulate their emotions and their behaviour (with some help in the early years). They will respond to normal classroom management, rules, rewards and sanctions. They can believe in themselves as a learner and believe that the teacher is able to teach and help them.

There is still a continuum of behaviour with securely attached children and young people - children will always break rules and check out boundaries - but in general, they are manageable and teachable.

The Learning Triangle

It's helpful in terms of understanding the connection between attachment and learning to use the framework of the Learning Triangle, developed by Heather Geddes (2006). She suggests that in any learning experience in the classroom, there is a triangle made up of the *teacher*, the *pupil* and the *task*. In order to learn, the child must trust the relationship with the teacher but be able to separate out from the teacher long enough to get on with the task independently. Securely attached children are able to do this, because they have learned to separate from their caregiver and to know that they are 'held in mind' (that the adult remembers them when not directly engaging with them). They can trust their own thinking and have space for learning and independence.

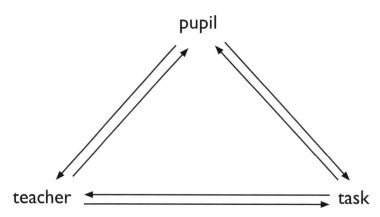

The Learning Triangle in school (Geddes 2006, p.4)

INSECURE ATTACHMENT

What is it and what does it look like in class?

Some children will not have had an experience of secure attachment with an empathic, responsive adult in their early years. There are many reasons for this, and some of them are discussed below. But the important information for you as the classroom teacher is that - for whatever reasons - some children and young people have learned other patterns of behaving and thinking. They have missed out on learning the skills needed to progress in class, and they don't believe they can learn or that the classroom is safe.

Factors which can adversely affect attachment

- Parental unavailability - addiction, depression, work, absence …
- Several moves of family home
- Separation or loss
- Mental, physical or emotional abuse
- Parental pre-birth stress, e.g. self-harm, domestic violence
- Alcohol or drug-taking during pregnancy
- Being a premature baby
- Bereavements in the family
- Migration and displacement
- Trauma and crisis in the family in the early years

For insecure attachment to develop, these factors often co-occur as a combination of risk factors for the growing child.

Creating safety

As mentioned in the previous chapter, these children need above all to feel safe in the classroom. There are practical ways that a teacher can help them with this.

CREATE A SUPPORTIVE ENVIRONMENT

*Try to create a supportive and cooperative classroom environment where difference is celebrated and pupils help each other. Include activities which work explicitly on teaching empathy, emotional understanding, and social skills. These activities will help all your pupils to develop their skills in these important areas, but are especially important for those with attachment difficulties (**and see** Chapters 6 **and** 8).*

CLASSROOM MANAGEMENT

√ Create class contracts which encourage the values of an inclusive classroom
'In this class, we give people extra time if they need it.'

√ Link your classroom rules to learning and safety. When creating them, ask, *'What rules do we need to make sure everyone feels safe and can learn at their best?'*

√ Remind pupils of the rules and the reasons for them, e.g. say explicitly, *'We agreed on the rules of this class together so that we can all learn as much as possible and feel safe doing it.'*

√ Have the rules clearly displayed, with visual representations if possible, and allow some pupils to have individual copies of rules on their desk or as a visual bookmark.

√ Practise acknowledging the need beneath any inappropriate behaviour e.g. *'You thought I had forgotten you, I hadn't …'* (and see Strategies for working with ambivalent-resistant children p.32 *for more ideas*).

√ Let pupils know what you want them to do and give them a positive reason for doing it, e.g. *'I need you to sit next to me now so that I can hear your opinions and check that you're doing your best work.'*

√ State positively what you want pupils to do rather than what you don't want them to do, e.g. *'Look at the board,'* rather than *'Don't turn around.'*

√ Try to state a positive intent in their behaviour but link to what you need them to do instead e.g. *'It's good that you want to join in the discussion but I just need you to remember to wait your turn'* (for more ideas on using classroom language positively see Chapter 7).

√ Use visual reminders such as traffic light cards to show that the class is generally on track with their work.

√ Use a system of visual reminders to indicate to the class the rules which apply to a particular activity, e.g. a blue card or a picture of the sea for showing the class it is OK to relax and talk, a red card for a Stop sign for showing it is time to stop talking and listen to the teacher.

MANAGING YOURSELF

√ Be aware of the state you are creating and the level of noise in the classroom - for many pupils, noise will create triggers. For example, if you are rushing around saying *'Stop, be quiet, listen to me,'* you are creating a whirlwind of energy which will cause agitation in pupils who are struggling to self-regulate. If you want quiet, stand calmly.

√ Take every opportunity to notice, name and comment on the appropriate behaviour when you see it, particularly with a child with attachment difficulties: *'Good waiting … you shared well …'*

GIVE CLEAR INSTRUCTIONS

√ Pupils with attachment difficulties may find it difficult to understand complex or indirect types of language so aim to keep your instructions clear and direct. For example, pupils may be confused by questions such as *'Who knows the answer?'* They may be waiting for the person called 'who' to answer.

Or they may wait for their own name to be called. Instead, ask -'*Simone, can you answer the question?*' Similarly, it would be better to say, '*Now write down tonight's homework task*', rather than something less direct, such as '*Now it's time for this week's challenge.*'

BE ORGANISED

√ Working in an organised environment will benefit many pupils with attachment difficulties as it will give them a sense of security and support their need for routine. For example, pupils often respond well to *visual input*, so a visual timetable, with pictures showing an outline of the day or the order of activities in the class, will be helpful. It can also be helpful to warn pupils about any forthcoming changes to their usual routine to help reduce anxiety.

AIM FOR A CALM ENVIRONMENT

Pupils with attachment difficulties thrive best in a calm classroom environment. Ensure that they are sitting in a comfortable place and position. They might need to sit in the same place in each lesson. You could also create a quiet place for pupils to go to when they become anxious, or simply turn their desk around so that they can avoid distraction. For younger children, use a small tent or furniture such as bookcases to create an area where pupils can work away from noise or other children.

ADAPT AND ACCOMMODATE

Notice when a pupil seems to feel safer and what type of activities seem to make them feel anxious. For example, multisensory activities can be helpful as they allow pupils to communicate more easily. When asking the class to work collaboratively, be aware that pairwork and group work can be difficult for some pupils, so sometimes you could allow them to complete activities quietly on their own. They need to learn to be alongside others before they can trust interactions with others.

HELPING PUPILS TO CALM DOWN

*Pupils with attachment difficulties are often stressed or anxious, or can become so quite easily if, for example, they find some work too difficult, or if the teacher corrects them, or if a routine changes without warning. They are often in their 'reptile brain' or switch easily into it - the oldest part of the brain that is activated when we feel threatened or sense danger, when our response is to fight, flee or freeze. This can lead to loss of concentration, lack of cooperation, or challenging behaviour. On those occasions, it's important to help the pupil calm down. Saying '**Calm down**' is not enough with children who have no strategies for doing so or haven't learned how to self-regulate their feelings. We need to help them to de-activate their stress system and activate the exploratory system which is needed for learning.*

√ When pupils are in a state of fight and flight, calm them down by giving them logical, left-brain tasks such as sorting, categorising, putting things in order, or tidying up. Don't try to talk to them about how they feel or why they behaved badly. Their brain needs to calm down first with logical, no-risk activities.

√ Teach pupils about the reptile brain and how we needed it in prehistoric times to recognise danger. With younger children, you can use a toy dinosaur or reptile. Older pupils can draw a cartoon representation and keep it on their desk. Bring out the toy or cartoon or point to it when the pupil becomes angry or upset as a gentle reminder for them to calm down and re-focus. Use this language with the whole class: '*We are in our reptile brains now and we need to get back into our thinking brains.*'

TYPES OF INSECURE ATTACHMENT

THE PUPIL WITH A PATTERN OF AMBIVALENT-RESISTANT ATTACHMENT

This is the child who is overly focused on the relationship with the teacher. In the Learning Triangle, we can see that the child can't separate out (away from the teacher) to get on with the learning task. Essentially, these children believe that if they lose the attention of the teacher, they will be forgotten. They probably couldn't predict their mother's response in their early years, and experienced inconsistency: sometimes they were remembered, sometimes they were not. They have learned that the only way to keep the adult's attention is to keep engaging them in the relationship.

THIS PATTERN WILL SHOW UP IN YOUR CLASS AS A PUPIL WHO -

- Is often very anxious, overly dependent on the teacher or teaching assistant
- Acts helpless and stuck without an adult constantly by their side
- Is unable to work independently
- Needs constant reassurance
- Is easily distracted from the task
- Is continually looking for the teacher: *'Miss, miss, I can't do it'*
- Gets upset very easily if they lose the teacher's attention
- Engages in arguments and discussions to avoid work
- Has good verbal language skills, more advanced than written skills, because they use their spoken language to keep your attention

STRATEGIES WHICH CAN HELP

√ Set small timed tasks which gradually wean the pupil away from dependence on your presence but show him that you have not forgotten him. This can be marked with younger children with egg-timers, and older pupils with the clock-face or their own watch. They need to learn to measure time.

√ Name their anxiety if you do not come back in the allocated time:

'Maybe you thought I had forgotten you, I hadn't.'

'I am sorry I didn't get back to you when we agreed, that must have been worrying for you. You probably thought I had forgotten you, but I hadn't.'

√ Choose tasks which follow a known pattern and are easy to start, so there can be no disagreements about not being able to do it. For example, you might start each task with a review of key words in the form of a word scramble.

√ Find a way to show you are noticing the pupil when you are not directly talking to them, e.g. thumbs up across the room, or set a behaviour target for the pupil, for example, *'I will focus on my own work'*. Give each pupil a card, or get them to make their own, with the title '*Catch me being good*' (or '*Getting it right*' for older pupils). Whenever you're walking around the class and you notice the pupil on task or behaving well, put a tick on the card.

√ If you have a teaching assistant, work with them on noticing and naming when the pupil is feeling anxious, and helping them to manage the anxiety.

√ Notice when you cannot bear their feelings of helplessness, and avoid the temptation to over-help. These children need to experience some frustration in order to develop their ability to problem-solve and learn. You can acknowledge their frustration but they need to be encouraged to trust their own thinking.

What this child has learned to expect from school
This pupil has essentially learned to believe that:
> *'If I don't continually check out the relationship and keep engaged with you directly, you will forget me and my needs will not be met.'*
>
> *'I can't trust in your availability and I will not show my need to separate and explore.'*

The Learning Triangle
This pupil is most preoccupied with the *relationship* part of the Learning Triangle: how to keep the teacher engaged. This means they often do not get onto the task part of the triangle.

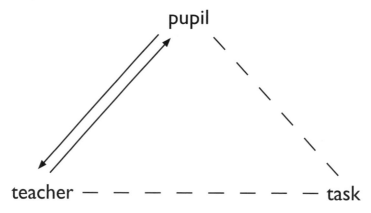

Learning Triangle: Resistant-Ambivalent Attachment

(Geddes 2006 p.97)

How they make us feel
Often as a teacher you will feel that nothing you do is every enough for these pupils. You might start out by feeling sympathetic and desperately wanting to help them, but over time you may become increasingly irritated by their constant demands. You can

Try saying, *'I know it can feel impossible to do this work without the teacher next to you. It can feel very frustrating when we are learning something new. You can trust your brain to do it though.'*

or

'Trust your own brain. What does it think?'

√   Name the anxiety they might be feeling when you have left them to attend to the needs of another pupil or pupils

'I know you find it hard to believe that I will remember you when I am not speaking to you on your own.'

'Maybe it's hard to believe that I haven't forgotten you when I am talking to the whole class, but I haven't'.

√   Above all, show the pupil that he is remembered at other times. This can be done by mentioning something which shows you were thinking about him outside the class. For example, if you know what football team he supports, you might say,

'I see Arsenal had a hard match on Saturday. I wondered if you watched it.'

Or comment on a general interest that may link the pupil to others in the class:

'I was in a shop at the weekend and I saw that the new DS game is out, the one you were talking about last week.'

√   Or, if you don't know much personal information about a pupil, you could show you remember him from your previous class:

'Last class Liam made an interesting point about the main character in this book.'

√   If you acknowledge that a pupil needs some way to keep contact with a teacher and you are his class teacher or form tutor, you could arrange to give him some special individual time. For example, you could let him help once a

feel that no amount of attention is ever enough, even though you recognise they need some kind of special attention. A sense of exasperation and of being manipulated often overwhelms you, followed by feeling guilty for becoming frustrated with such a helpless child.

Some adults feel such sympathy that they can't bear the helplessness, and this results in doing most of the work for the pupil. If you are not careful, such pupils elicit the 'Velcro' response: someone who is continually at their side doing all their thinking for them. And this response from staff means that such pupils don't learn to trust their own thinking and to see themselves as able to learn.

Words staff use around pupils with this pattern of behaviour

Teachers tend to use the following words around these pupils:

Needs

The main need of this pupil is to know that you remember them when you are not with them. When they realise this, they can start to separate away from you and trust their own thinking enough to get on with a learning task. We learn to think by being thought about, so they need to have their anxiety understood and contained. By contained I mean recognised by an adult, thought about and the feelings named if appropriate. These pupils need to trust that their relationship (with you as their teacher) will be still there when they are doing a task independently.

week with something at lunchtime. It would be important to make sure that he knows the exact day and time. Without this, he is likely to come on other days, and ask if he can help at other times. It needs to be made clear to him that he has a set time and that is the time to come. You can help him to manage this anxiety (about being forgotten) by referring to your meetings at other times. For example, you might say after class,

'I'm really pleased you are going to help me to sort that cupboard out on Tuesday lunchtime. I need help with that.'

√ By letting the child know that he is genuinely needed and that his help is valued, the time together will become more important and satisfying for him than time he used to get by manipulation. But be careful about being drawn into this with a pupil, if you are new and concentrating on your teaching: you might need to ask another member of staff about this, and for some support.

DEVELOPING RELATIONSHIPS WITH PEERS

√ Use any opportunity you can to help the pupil develop relationships with peers and to move away from a preoccupation with you, the teacher.

√ For example, find out if your school has a peer mentoring or buddy system or try to get him involved in a club at lunchtime.

PAUSE FOR THOUGHT

Do you recognise this pattern in any of your pupils?
Do you have a strategy which works?
Can you choose one of the strategies that might be new to you, to try with your pupil?

THE PUPIL WITH A PATTERN OF AVOIDANT ATTACHMENT

This is the child who has learned not to seek attachment and attention from the adult. If a child looks for attachment and validation from their caregiver and doesn't get it, and instead gets rebuffed, ignored or rejected, the child might learn not to ask, but instead to try to manage things alone. The avoidant attachment pattern means that a child has learned not to look for help and support from adults, so will tend to not ask for help in class and reject any attempts to form relationships directly. It can develop if the child has a -

- Depressed parent
- An emotionally unavailable parent
- Controlling parent, who can't cope with the child's needs
- An overly-anxious parent: the pattern can also develop as a defence in response to overwhelming anxiety from a parent

THIS PATTERN WILL SHOW UP IN A CLASS AS THE PUPIL WHO -

- Denies the need for support and help from teacher or teaching assistant
- Doesn't want the teacher or teaching assistant to stand in close proximity
- Shows apparent indifference to anxiety in a new situation
- May refuse to work with a teaching assistant
- Wants to do the task completely independently
- May get frustrated and rip up their work rather than ask for help
- Shows limited use of verbal communication which would involve building a relationship
- Shows limited creativity, because that might involve taking risks in learning which they cannot control
- Reacts badly to direct, verbal praise

STRATEGIES

√ Stop trying to make a direct relationship with the pupil. If something is not working, don't do more of it: do something different!

√ Reassurance often doesn't work because it involves accepting the relationship. Try simply naming what is happening. You might say:

'You want to do it on your own, without our help.'

'What do you think we can do to get this finished?'

√ Notice when the pupil is engaged and use these kinds of tasks to check in with him. You can then comment on the tasks using depersonalised language. For example,

'Number 3 is a bit more difficult. There is an example on the board".

This is different to, *'I see you have found number 3 a bit difficult. Let me show you another example on the board'.*

√ Notice how your pupil relates to his peers. Sometimes avoidant children are happy to work with particular peers. Sit him with helpful ones.

√ Give praise differently. Maybe he can accept praise in a letter home, or a private word, or a tick on his book. He may need to learn to accept certificates in private in an envelope before he can accept anything in public. You could try just leaving them in his tray with a message.

√ Comment on the task - *'That's a well written story'* - rather than the child's efforts - *'I'm very pleased with it.'* Or let him own the praise - *'You must be proud of yourself.'*

√ Find ways to acknowledge his work in public in different ways. For example, you might take a picture of it or scan it for a newsletter or wall display.

What this child has learned to expect from school

These pupils expect rebuff and rejection from adults, and have learned to believe that:

'If I look for your attention, I will get rejected, so I will not seek out any relationship with the teacher. I will do it on my own.'

'I fear my need of you and I will not show you my need for comfort and protection.'

The Learning Triangle

This pupil finds refuge in the *task*. This is the safe part of the Learning Triangle for him. The relationship part is not safe and needs to be avoided.

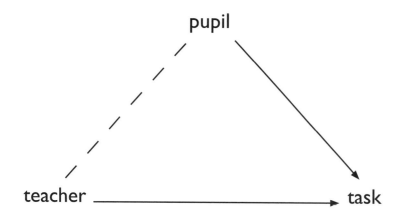

Learning Triangle: Avoidant Attachment

(Geddes 2006, p.77)

How they make us feel

With this child you might feel as if you are not needed, useless, rejected and not at all important. For many of us who want to be needed and to offer support and help,

- √ Sometimes it can help to suggest that work is stored in a temporary box or carton, and then reviewed after a period of time to see if it can be kept, worked on or thrown away. This can be an A4 box folder or something similar. Set up a system of looking at the work at the end of the week to decide what to do with it. It allows the pupil control of the work.

- √ Plan tasks which allow him to work alongside another child or adult and work indirectly. When planning your lesson, you can choose methods and activities based on the needs you have recognised.

- √ Decide to build in some choice where possible with the work.

  'We need to learn these words. You can choose to do the word search first, or start with the matching exercise.'

- √ Organise group work with different roles and information. Pupils with this pattern of behaviour often respond to having a clear role and responsibility in a group of peers. Having a role in a smaller group can make the interactions feel safer as the child can focus on the task element of their role and doesn't have to engage directly in a relationship with the teacher. They might, for example, research some information for a presentation, and other pupils can present the findings to the teacher and the class.

- √ Plan to notice and deal with your own feelings of uselessness. Avoid further rejection if possible. This may involve talking it through with a trusted colleague.

- √ The child needs to learn to eventually make use of the relationship with the teaching staff so that they can make real progress with the task. In this way, they are far more likely to maximise their true learning potential.

  'You have nearly finished that on your own and perhaps Ms A can look at it with you.'

these are very painful feelings. We begin by feeling sympathetic and can eventually become angry and start to reject the pupil. We might feel *'If they don't want to engage with me, there is nothing I can do.'* The problem arises because we usually want to 'have a chat and discuss how we can help' and this involves offering the most dangerous thing for the pupil - the relationship.

Words staff use around pupils with this pattern of behaviour

Teachers often use these words around such pupils:

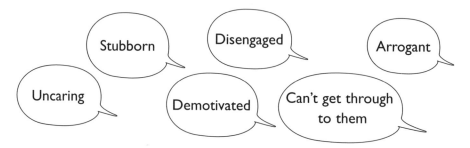

Needs

The pupil with an avoidant attachment pattern needs to feel in control and autonomous, to not give the teacher the power over him to hurt him or make him feel powerless by knowing something better than him. In essence, they need the teacher to understand that being noticed can feel dangerous and that they do not want to feel overwhelmed or taken over by the relationship.

PAUSE FOR THOUGHT

Do you recognise this pattern in any of your pupils?
Do you have a strategy which works?
Can you choose one of the strategies that might be new to you,
to try with your pupil?

THE PUPIL WITH A PATTERN OF DISORGANISED ATTACHMENT

Children with an insecure, disorganised style of attachment usually come from chaotic, damaged backgrounds, suffering severe neglect, violence and/or abuse. They can be the most distressing to work with and to try to teach. They seem erratic in their responses and can display very distressing behaviours which put them or others at risk, for example, banging their heads against the wall when frustrated or after being corrected. It's not always possible to see the immediate trigger to their extreme behaviour. Such pupils are very difficult to support into learning and the most challenging to respond to, but fortunately constitute the smallest percentage of pupils in the insecure attachment group. They often develop controlling/punitive behaviour towards the parent and other adults, and they have very impoverished relationships, even with their peers.

Children and young people with this pattern of erratic responses and distressing behaviours can disrupt lessons and cause upset to the teacher and other pupils.

....

THIS PATTERN WILL SHOW UP IN A CLASS AS THE PUPIL WHO -

- Changes rapidly from being very agitated to 'switched off'. One minute they might be loudly demanding your attention, and the next, telling you they don't need you and to go away
- Gets very frustrated and show this by banging their heads against the wall
- Runs around uncontrollably
- Runs out of class unexpectedly
- Explodes into temper for no apparent reason
- Can be very abusive to the other children in the class
- Can be very abusive to the teacher, rubbishing their attempts to teach

TEACHING STRATEGIES

√   Work with other staff to support each other. It can be difficult for you as the teacher to plan to meet your pupil's needs because they respond differently from week to week.

√   The key task in working with these children and young people is to acknowledge the strain put on us by their chaotic behaviour. When working with them, we can experience high levels of anxiety, not being sure how they will react on a day-to-day basis. Unexpected eruptions, aggression, persistent refusal to co-operate or focus on the lesson, an apparent lack of respect and empathy towards others are wearying experiences when it is every day. Such behaviour attacks the thinking capacity of the teacher. We need to see our task as maintaining and restoring our own capacity to think, and then subsequently, the child's.

√   As a class teacher, you need to be aware of who else can help, and get involved in any regular meetings with other professionals working with this pupil. If you are not invited to these meetings, make sure you know what strategies have been discussed to support the child so that you don't feel alone.

√   Don't be afraid to say you are finding it difficult to cope. These pupils may need a different provision in smaller group settings and/or one-to-one support. There are several strategies which can help create the safety they need (*as discussed on* p.28). In addition, many of the strategies which are often suggested for children on the autistic spectrum can help provide some structure and safety for pupils with this pattern of behaviour as well. The following provides further options.

√   Have clear routines and structures and use visual timetables if appropriate to show the daily routines.

What this child has learned to expect from school

This pupil has learned to believe that:

'The world is a dangerous, chaotic place and isn't safe.'

'No-one and nothing can be trusted.'

'I will not need you, needing you is dangerous.'

'I cannot explore the world, I am too busy ensuring I am safe.'

The Learning Triangle

Because the only consistent thing about these pupils is their lack of consistency, they do not seem to have any pattern in relation to the Learning Triangle. Sometimes they engage in the relationship, sometimes they engage in the class but mostly they seem disconnected from both learning and relationships. They can't focus on the relationship or the task because their main preoccupation is checking that they are safe.

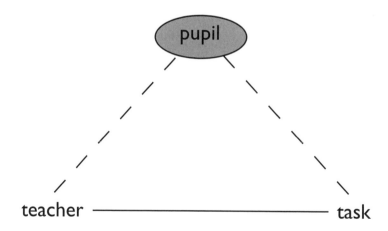

Learning Triangle: Disorganised/Disorientated Attachment

(Geddes 2006, p.115)

√   Flag up any changes to routine in advance if possible, and reflect back how catastrophic a change might feel (and that measures have been put in place to help).

    For example, use visual icons on your board to show the order of the lesson and if necessary, give the child their own icons to know the structure.

√   If you have a teaching assistant, work closely with them to make sure the pupil knows the routine and any changes in routine. If there are going to be many changes in a day - for example you are going to be absent or the normal routine will be disrupted by a whole school event such as sports day, discuss with your SENCO and others to find a safe place for the pupil to go to.

√   If that is not possible, have a back-up plan in case they erupt in class or give them a timeout card to use. They may need, for example, to head for their safe place where they can do simple worksheets and calm down.

√   Transitions and endings need to be carefully planned and acknowledged (see Chapter 5 *on transitions*).

√   Discuss with the child the best place to sit in class. For some this will be near the teacher, for others this will be somewhere they can see everyone in the class: or it might be near a door, so they can indicate if they need help and need to escape.

√   You may need to have a bank of logical, left-brain, concrete tasks such as sorting, ordering, categorising, filling in and colouring in. These tasks will soothe their anxiety and provide some kind of logical order. Tasks which are more open-ended, involve metaphorical thinking and creativity may be quite frightening for these pupils, and having a back-up, a logical, less stressful task, can help.

How they make us feel

These are the children we will feel most helpless about. Generally we have feelings of helplessness and overwhelming feelings of hopelessness. They can make us feel fearful, anxious, hurt and sad. These feelings can lead to rejecting, punitive approaches. We react angrily or push them away because we feel so useless in our attempts to help. These children however are a small minority, and may not be in mainstream classes.

Words staff use around pupils with this pattern of behaviour

Teachers often use these words around these pupils:

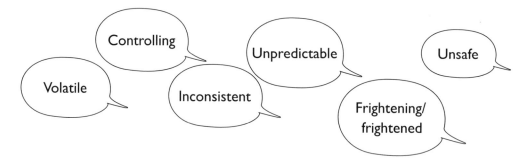

Needs

The main need of these children and young people is for basic safety. They are, in fact, focused on survival. They have a constant need to be hyper-vigilant and look out for dangers, real and imagined. It can help to remember that much of their difficult behaviour is prompted by fear and overwhelming anxiety. They quite simply have no space in their minds to think, learn or engage in relationships. So in school they need to have a strong, containing structure around them which can withstand their overwhelming, painful feelings and enable them to feel safe. They need to know that there is a structure to school and learning, which they may eventually learn to rely on. They may have experienced ridicule, humiliation and denigration from adults, and will continually need to be shown and reassured that this will not be the case in school.

√   Use activities which allow these pupils to work on the idea of being 'found', put back together. For example, finding a missing link, putting something back into the picture, completing a puzzle, joining the dots and so on (see Ch. 8).

√   Take a small, step-by-step approach. Find something your pupil is good at and allow them to spend some time on this when they are out of other classes. This needs to be part of an agreed plan. It is not a 'reward' for bad behaviour, but an acknowledgement that they are still a capable person even when they have been unable to manage themselves in the classroom. Take the longer view and notice small amounts of progress. It can be all too easy to lose sight of the bigger picture with these pupils.

NOTICE TRIGGERS

Some children and young people with this type of attachment difficulty will be very sensitive to certain sensory triggers. It can help to start keeping a checklist of what interests the pupil and what triggers positive or negative reactions. For example:

SENSORY INTERESTS (positive):
- spinning or revolving objects
- lining things up
- touching or smelling things

SENSORY TRIGGERS (negative):
- bright lights and colours
- loud noises

PAUSE FOR THOUGHT

Do you recognise this pattern in any of your pupils?
Do you have a strategy which works?
Can you choose one of the strategies that might be new to you, to try with your pupil?

CONTAINMENT

Bion (1962) writes about the need for the adult to provide 'containment' of the overwhelming feelings an infant might have. In school, the feelings around pupils who are not coping well can threaten to overwhelm us. It can be difficult to acknowledge when any of us are feeling overwhelmed as we believe we should be able to cope, that we need to be 'strong' in order to set a good example. And yes, we do need to be able to manage our feelings: but that isn't the same as ignoring and suppressing them. If feelings are suppressed or ignored, in an attempt to appear 'strong' and able to cope, they will often come to the surface in some other way, in stress-related illnesses for example, or irritation and outbursts.

We need to be able to recognise the feelings, 'digest' them, and think about them without panicking. It isn't just the children's feelings which need to be contained, but also our own. This is why support groups are so important.

For pupils with a pattern of disorganised attachment, the school building can come to represent a secure physical base, and provide containment. It is a place where:

- **rules and boundaries are clear**
- **routines are established**
- **in general, the day is predictable**
- **the roles of adult and child are clear**

It's important to remember that even if these pupils seem to hate the rules and kick against them, they are looking, however unconsciously, to be 'contained'. In fact, school for many children is the safest place to act out and protest. The boundaries in school may seem safer and stronger than at home, and therefore need to be tested, and to stick. We must make sure as staff we don't get caught up in splitting.

BOX 4 SPLITTING

Children with attachment difficulties often polarise people and opinions. Adults working with the child can find themselves blaming each other, vehemently disagreeing about what to do or feeling that they are the only person who understands and is helping the child.

It is important to notice if this is happening around a child that you teach. It can be understood as the defence mechanism of *splitting*, a way in which the child deals with extreme anxiety.

Being able to recognise that people are made up of different parts and that that is OK, is an important part of a child's development. Securely attached children learn to realise that their parent or caregiver can love them and can still be cross with them sometimes. In class therefore, such pupils will understand that the teacher can sometimes be annoyed or shout, but this is not a catastrophe and does not mean they hate the children.

However insecurely attached children find it hard to believe they can be made up of different parts. They talk about being 'good' or 'bad'. This view of the world can transfer to the behaviour of the adults working with the child, who begin to polarise in their views of the child and to experience the splitting process, unable to focus on working together to find ways to support the student. So it's important that we adults don't fall into this polarised view of the world, or re-create it ourselves in response.

If you can be aware of splitting when it happens, you can work to minimise it by consciously not taking up an extreme position in relation to other staff and to collaborating together to find a solution, rather than getting stuck in a blaming frame of mind. It can help to stop thinking in mutually exclusive ways such as *'Either we do A or we do B'*. Try instead to reframe the thinking as, *'How can we do A and B, or the best of both A and B?'*

> **PAUSE FOR THOUGHT**
>
> *Have you noticed yourself or other members of staff in strong disagreement about the best way to understand and work with a student who has challenging behaviour?*
> *Could this be a sign of splitting? What first step could you take to undoing this?*

PLAY

Many children with attachment difficulties have not fully developed their ability to play. This is important, because learning to play gives children many of the skills they need to learn in a classroom. It can be helpful to remember how a young child learns to play through the developmental stages cited by Winnicott (1971):

- Playing with the mother, not separate
- Playing with self, toes, fingers and so on
- Playing with an object, for example, a blanket, a soft toy
- Playing alone, but in the mother's presence
- Playing alongside another child (a stage often seen in nursery school, where two children will be playing, for example, in the 'home' area, but not with each other, alongside each other)
- Inviting another child to join in your play
- Being invited in to play another child's game and being able to follow their rules and inventions

(*and see* Delaney, 2008 p.130-131)

We can see that in order to learn in a classroom environment, pupils need to have reached the final stage of play development, that of 'playing' by someone else's rules - the teacher's, the school's, or society's in general. Many of the pupils discussed in this book - even those in secondary school - have not reached this stage of play. They cheat if they're not winning, they can't wait for a turn, they can't bear to lose and they argue about rules if they can't follow them. This inability to play by others' rules can be seen in class when a pupil is:

- Unable to take turns in class or in their group
- Spoils things for others, for example by cheating, when they are not winning
- Insists on going first in games: sulking or getting angry if they are not picked
- Tries to take over in group work with their peers and doesn't listen to other people's ideas
- Refuses to participate if their group overrides their decisions or does not choose their ideas
- Argues about rules and instructions and then tries to change them if they are losing or get it wrong, saying for example, *'Well, when I've done this before, we didn't do it like this.'*

This kind of behaviour can be particularly frustrating for you if you teach secondary age pupils who we generally assume have learned these skills. Many haven't had the opportunity to learn these play skills and are developmentally at a younger age than their chronological age, as I mentioned back on p.16.

STRATEGIES WHICH CAN HELP

✓ Take any opportunities you can find to include play and games in your classroom. Don't feel guilty for doing this.

✓ Tasks and games can be designed for our classes to help these children learn to play and express their feelings in a safe way.

✓ Games and tasks can give a child a chance to express hostile feelings towards the teacher and learning. Games offer the opportunity to 'defeat' the teacher by learning, rather than by 'not-learning'.

✓ Through guessing, competitive and turn-taking games, the child can learn to bear not knowing an answer and feeling frustrated - key skills in learning.

✓ Pupils will not necessarily play games properly at first. Don't give up on the game. Stop it and ask them what rules are needed to make this game safe and fun for everyone. Re-start the game and refer often to link with rules and safety.

SUMMARY

Attachment theory, as initially developed by John Bowlby and Mary Ainsworth, can be a useful model for thinking about the needs of seemingly unteachable children and young people. In this chapter I've given some of the ways of identifying patterns of behaviour that might indicate a particular pupil had attachment difficulties, and by differentiating between the various styles of attachment, provided some strategies to help each group of pupils begin to engage with learning.

▷ Infants are pre-programmed to develop *attachment behaviour* and 'use' their *attachment figure* as a *secure base* from which to develop and explore.

▷ Children with a *secure early attachment experience* can readily develop skills for learning. Their relationship to the teacher and to tasks is in balance.

▷ Children with *insecure attachment experiences* may be unable to learn, as they are too pre-occupied with checking out their relationship with the teacher or they will only focus on the task and not allow help. The *Learning Triangle* between pupil/teacher and task is skewed in some way (Geddes 2006).

▷ Teachers often come to represent *key attachment figures* in these children's lives.

▷ Before thinking about strategies to manage these children, we need to think about their *underlying needs* and the experiences they have not yet had.

▷ Don't collude with their patterns of behaviour. For example, if they exhibit an avoidant pattern, make every effort not to reject them or to be 'over-bright' in your dealing with them.

▷ Children with an *ambivalent-resistant* insecure attachment style need to learn to separate from the adult in small steps and to pay attention to the task.

▷ Children with an *avoidant insecure attachment style* need to learn to trust the relationship with an adult, but through engagement with a task.

▷ Children with a *disorganised attachment style* are the most chaotic and difficult to teach. However, they represent a small percentage of 'unteachable' children and young people. For them, it is imperative we develop and work with a strong network and clear, consistent routines to provide them with essential safety. Schools can provide the experience of what Bion called the 'containment' of potentially overwhelming feelings for these children - both emotionally, through routines and relationships, and physically, through the buildings.

▷ At school children have the opportunity to experience new ways of relating which offer a 'second-chance' at developing secure attachment patterns.

▷ Children will sometimes turn against the adult who has supported them most. This is a testing of the relationship and its boundaries. It should not be seen as rejection, and the adult needs to resist the desire to give up working with them. Equally, as staff, we need to work together, and not 'split' or polarise when there are strongly divided feelings about a pupil.

▷ Many of these children have not yet learned to play with others and by other people's rules. Using play and games in the classroom can help them to develop play skills needed for learning.

Chapter 4

Challenging behaviours - meet the pupils

The three types of insecure attachment patterns described in the previous chapter give a useful framework for understanding the difficulties of some of the pupils in our classes. Often as a teacher the first way of noticing that a pupil is having problems is through their challenging behaviour or apparent blocks to learning in class. In this chapter, we'll look in more detail at some patterns of behaviour and reactions to learning which might be a sign of attachment difficulties. I'll describe:

- **the *behaviour* you might notice or witness from a pupil**
- **the *needs* that may be underlying or driving their behaviour and**
- **the *strategies* which can help the individual pupil**

Some of these strategies will of course have been mentioned in the previous chapter - as essentially what I'll be describing here are variations on the three types of insecure attachment pattern, although perhaps they won't appear that way at first sight. For each type of behaviour, you will see a short description, potential thoughts about what it might be showing us about the child's unmet needs, and the possible teaching strategies you can try. I hope the chapter will help you develop your curiosity about what's going on behind whatever behaviour you're finding particularly challenging at the moment.

Remember that every pupil is different and there will always be a trial-and-error approach to finding the 'right' strategy: but the ones suggested are designed to try to meet the possible needs shown to us by the behaviours I described in the last chapter.

Ambivalent-resistant attachment
- hypervigilant, not able to settle and focus
- recreating violence and aggression to keep the adult engaged
- helplessness to ensure the adult's constant support and reassurance
- manipulation of the adults to ensure needs met and not forgotten
- continual challenge and disagreement, to keep the adult engaged in defending and explaining their position
- avoidance of work by continually engaging the adult in the relationship, often through charm and social conversation

Patterns of insecure attachment

Avoidant attachment
- omnipotence, acting all-knowing and wanting complete control to avoid not knowing, and to keep away from feelings of humiliation
- perfectionism, trying to do everything right first time, seeming very compliant and generally not attracting the teacher's attention in any way

Disorganised attachment
- running away, often out of class and sometimes out of the school building
- lying and being unable to accept that the adults can cope with and respond appropriately to the truth
- rubbishing their own work, that of other pupils and the efforts of the teacher to help

Some types of behaviour might be difficult to categorise, as there may only be subtle differences in the pattern. For example, a pupil who is acting very aggressively and argumentatively toward you could be trying to keep contact with you as reassurance that you won't forget them (ambivalent-resistant attachment) or could be unable to regulate their rage towards the world in general because it is so frightening to them (disorganised attachment).

Don't worry: remember that this type of work involves a 'trial and error' approach. It isn't always necessary to have the exact theoretical label for a pupil's behaviour. It is more important to look out for patterns and to wonder about the underlying needs. Then you can try out strategies which are focused on attempting to meet those needs, rather than responding only to the observed behaviour. Your attempts to understand the child's needs and empathise with them, and willingness to try something different, will be invaluable to the pupil.

▎ THE HYPERVIGILANT PUPIL

'Potential danger is all around'

This pupil is on high alert for danger at all times. In class they appear unable to focus, continually turning round, interfering with other pupils' tasks and equipment, sometimes roaming restlessly around the room, over-reacting to sudden noises - even at times running out of the room.

They are often diagnosed with ADHD and of course exhibit many of the signs and 'symptoms' that could lead to that description. But their main need is to be reassured about safety in the environment, in learning and especially in the relationship with the teacher. If the pupil seems to seek proximity and safety from you, the teacher, it's likely that they are showing an ambivalent-resistant attachment pattern.

However, hypervigilance can also be a sign of a disorganised attachment pattern if the child finds the whole environment and people in it threatening. The difference is that the child with a disorganised attachment pattern will not usually seek or gain reassurance from contact with the teacher. They will often only feel safe with a figure of high authority, such as the headteacher.

NEEDS

If you think the pupil's hypervigilance is reassured by contact with you, the main needs of this child are likely to be:

▷ To feel safe and secure
▷ To believe you (the teacher) like(s) them as a person even when their behaviour is annoying - these pupils often perceive criticism as a sign they are not liked

STRATEGIES

√   Encourage study buddies, pupils who can work together and help each other: use smaller groups for group work. Sit the pupil next to good role models who will not attempt to distract for fun.

√   Use visual memory aids for learning points, for example, a visual timetable, or, for behaviour, a traffic light system on the wall.

√   When giving instructions, ask for and get examples.

√   Let the pupil doodle to relieve anxiety: let them underline a text as you are reading, to help them focus.

√   Use individual laminated whiteboards so that pupils can show their answers rather than having to choose when to speak

√   Have a Worry Box where pupils can privately write down any worries they want the teacher to know about

√   Encourage a *stop, wait and count to ten approach* and mindful breathing. Teach the pupil to step back mentally, breathe in through nose for four, hold, breathe out through mouth for four. Allow them to stand up and stretch and look around to assess safety

√   Allow the pupil to work with headphones on or to imagine wearing headphones. Think with the pupil about the best place to sit - near a door or at the back where they can see everyone, but away from distractions such as windows, heaters. Allow the pupil to go to a designated area if the classroom is getting too stressful, so that they can cool down

2 THE PUPIL WHO RECREATES VIOLENCE

'Attack is the best form of defence'

If a pupil has lived with violence, they may unconsciously recreate what they are used to. The process of transference, where they re-enact relationships from their past with the key figures in school, can come into play here. Teachers might find it difficult to understand that children who have experienced violence and know the pain, turn to violence. It can be difficult not to become the angry aggressor yourself in these situations. If you find yourself being pulled into a certain way of behaving, for example getting very angry with a child who comes from a volatile background, you might be getting caught up in the counter-transference - where we start behaving as the person we remind the pupil of (see p.15).

The aggressive child might also be presenting a disorganised attachment pattern, particularly if the aggression seems unpredictable, happens in many different circumstances and is aimed towards other peers and adults. However, if the aggression is primarily aimed at you, their teacher and seems to involve a need to keep you continually engaged with them, it is more likely to be an example of an ambivalent-resistant attachment.

NEEDS

The main needs of this pupil are:

▷ **To feel safe**
▷ **To have a different experience of an adult responding to their anger or aggression**
▷ **To learn that they will be heard/understood without resorting to violence**
▷ **To have their feeling validated and understood - they may have had good reason to feel angry in another place, and at another time**

STRATEGIES

It is important to break the pattern of re-enacting aggression and to be able to use de-escalation strategies with these pupils. De-escalation strategies include the following:

√   Don't get drawn into the pattern of becoming the aggressor.

√   If necessary move to another quieter place and describe what is happening for you: *'When you are shouting I can't hear what you want to say, I need you to calm down.'*

√   Be aware of your own state, how you're standing, breathing and talking. Breathing deep in your belly will regulate and lower your voice. Stand balanced on both feet.

√   Be clear about the outcome you need and don't get sidetracked by angry feelings.
'I need you to move over here now so you can get on with your work.'

√   Avoid where possible being drawn in by secondary behaviour, e.g. when a pupil sighs and mutters/swears, but does what is asked.

√   Try to avoid direct public confrontations when you are feeling angry. Develop techniques, such as mindful breathing, which allow you to take a step back and calm yourself down before trying to resolve the issue with an angry child.

√   Address the behaviour rather than the person or your opinion of the person.

√   Match voice, tone, body language, key words.

√   If students go off task and start misbehaving, try to avoid a confrontation.

Instead, redirect their attention back to the task: e.g. *'You've made a good start on your essay. The first paragraph has got some great ideas. How are you going to develop them in the next part?'*

√ Say what you want to happen, not what you don't want to happen. Use short sentences and logical sequencing when giving instructions to a student who is upset.

√ Stack up things which you know the other person has to agree with.

'You're upset about this and you've stayed behind and we all want to get this resolved …' As you are saying these things, the angry person is inwardly agreeing and calming down.

Use 'we' where possible, and refer to any previous agreement: *'We agreed on …'*

√ Pace their objections and acknowledge them: this is not the same as agreeing with them. *'I understand that you think this is unfair, and you do need to stay behind to finish this work ...'*

√ Don't make idle threats or offer consequences which you can't follow through on.

√ Discuss the issue, not your interpretation of it. It's easy to ascribe our own motives to another person's behavior. This is only mind-reading.

√ Allow for silence, beyond the point at which you are comfortable, and really listen. Ask yourself *'Am I listening to understand, or listening to reply?'*

√ Use open-ended questions to elicit information. *'How …?' 'What …?' 'Tell me …?'* rather than *'Why …?'* which can put people on the defensive.

√ Be prepared to try to understand the student's map of the world and show curiosity in it. You will establish better rapport and get better outcomes.

3 THE HELPLESS PUPIL

'I can't do it on my own'

The helpless child is one who seems unable to work on their own without the intervention and support of an adult. In class they:

- often call you over and ask for help even for work they can do.
- can react angrily when they don't get help, or get very upset, crying and turning against the teacher for not helping them.
- seem to have low self-esteem and little belief in themselves as a learner.
- rarely finish work.

NEEDS

The main needs of this pupil are:

▷ to learn to separate out from the adult
▷ to trust their own thinking
▷ to understand that they can learn, and to bear the feelings brought on by not knowing something

STRATEGIES

Above all, don't collude with the pupil's pattern of helplessness and avoid getting drawn into believing they can't work on their own.

√ Use the phrase, *'Trust your own thinking …'*

√ Acknowledge the pain of helplessness for them: *'I know it feels terrible when you can't do something.'*

√ Notice and praise times when they do succeed independently, no matter how small the progress.

√ Use commentaries which notice the skills they are practicing such as *'You're getting stronger every day at trusting your own thinking …'*

√ Allow for painful silences when you are waiting for this pupil to answer or do the work. Try not to jump in too soon with advice and help

√ Set small manageable goals and offer a step-by-step approach to completing the goal.

4 THE 'MANIPULATIVE' PUPIL

'I need to make sure several people meet my needs'

This is the pupil who seems to work their way around the teachers, often getting one teacher very involved in their issues and problems and then moving on to another when not getting what they want. Teachers sometimes find themselves arguing with each other, 'splitting' around the child, and taking up opposing positions. In class these pupils:

- might not be getting on with their own work because they are too preoccupied by maintaining a relationship with you and any other adults in the room, by getting you 'on their side'.
- may lie about other teachers' involvement and behaviour related to their work and communication with other staff (*see p.82 on lying*).
- spend a lot of time telling you long involved stories about perceived slights and problems with other staff.

NEEDS

These pupils seem to be unable to trust that one adult can meet their needs and understand their situation. They need to communicate their needs to as many adults as possible in case some of them are unreliable. They seek out relationships but often move on to another member of staff if they sense rejection or criticism. They need to understand that sometimes an adult can be annoyed with them, for example, but will still care about them and will not reject them because of a disagreement.

STRATEGIES

Above all, work with other staff to ensure that you are all informed about the reality of the situation. Don't assume that the pupil's version is true when it involves another member of staff.

√   Acknowledge the need and ask these questions:

   'Why has this child had to learn to manipulate in order to get their needs met?'
   'How can we meet their needs in other ways?'

√   Possibly have a class book to record any extra interactions with the pupil and monitor how much time is spent with each teacher.

√   Give some special time if possible, but plan this with other staff.

√   Give the pupil ways to attract your attention which do not require them to continually engage you in private conversation in class, e.g. worry book, journal, a card on their desk which can be turned over when they need help

√   Raise awareness with other staff who dismiss the child as 'manipulative' and challenge yourself and them to understand why this child has had to learn to behave this way; contrast with a child from a secure and supportive background, who can freely trust adults to look after him.

5 THE OVERLY ARGUMENTATIVE PUPIL

'I have to ensure justice and fairness for everyone at all times'

This student has a heightened sense of justice and fairness and will try to continually engage you in disputes about the fairness of your actions in class. They will often intervene on another student's behalf and get involved in other people's business. In class you will often hear cries of 'It's not fair - why aren't they getting punished?', or 'Why is it still going on … ?' This extreme and narrow focus on fairness is sometimes like that of a much younger child. Essentially these children have not passed through a developmental stage known as constancy, when a child understands that people have different parts that are integrated in the whole being. They still don't understand for example that a parent can be tired and irritated at times, but also still love them and care for them. The parent moves through different states and feelings but remains the same person.

It can also be another example of the psychological defence of splitting, the process of viewing something or someone as all good or all bad, rather than understanding that real life is usually a mixture of both (see p.51). This 'all or nothing' extreme approach makes it difficult for these children to understand that it is impossible to be 100% fair and consistent with everyone all the time.

NEEDS

The basic need for this type of student is to understand that there is a middle ground between two extremes. They need to understand, for example, that you can be annoyed by their behaviour but still care about them or that if you give another child some extra time one day, it doesn't mean you are ignoring them.

STRATEGIES

√ Avoid being drawn into justifying your decisions and a discussion on fairness. Such pupils will always find examples to prove you wrong if you begin by saying, *'It is fair, everyone gets the same treatment'*: you might be trying for consistency but this pupil will often counter your defence with an example when you were not consistent!

√ Acknowledge their objections: *'I know you think it's unfair,'* and remind them of the rules if necessary. *'John needs some extra help today and our rule is that everyone gets extra time if they need it.'*

√ Remind of the meaning of fairness in your class: *'Fairness is not everyone getting the same, it's everyone getting what they need.'*

√ Remind them gently that you are the adult in charge of the room and welfare of others: *'I will worry about the other pupils, and you just need to focus on yourself.'*

√ This is a typical of children and young people with an ambivalent attachment pattern, and they need to be reminded that you have not forgotten them if someone else is getting extra help.

√ If you can, use inclusive language to resolve potential conflicts and keep the focus on learning: *'How can we resolve this problem? How can we make sure learning takes place?'*

√ Take every opportunity to show examples of the different sides of a person's personalities and how different feelings can exist in the same person (*see p.138 on polar opposites*).

6 THE PUPIL WHO CONTINUALLY AVOIDS WORK

'If I get involved in the task, the teacher might forget me or I will not know what to do and feel vulnerable'

You will have students who are experts at avoiding doing any work and it can show up in different ways:

- the pupil who is socially very adept, keeping you engaged in conversation, asking you about yourself, discussing recent events with great interest, often seeming quite charming
- the pupil who is the 'class clown' - making jokes, always cheerful and upbeat
- the pupil who acts helpless and continually tells you that the work is too hard
- the pupil who provokes constant arguments and discussion with you

In essence, all of these students are spending time engaging with the relationship between the teacher and themselves, and not getting onto their work.

NEEDS

These students are often preoccupied with the relationship and do not trust their own independent thinking. They may need to keep themselves safe from feelings of vulnerability and not knowing something that engagement in the task might bring. They may be unable to acknowledge their feelings of anxiety with regard to their ability to do the task and so will distract by engaging the teacher in different ways.

STRATEGIES

The main thing is to recognise when a student is avoiding the task. It isn't always obvious in a large class. Socially adept avoiders of work often don't get picked up. They might not be causing a great problem and can be quite charming and interesting to talk to.

√   Try to understand why they are not doing the work. Check they know how to do it and that it is not too hard or too easy.

√   Keep the focus on the work wherever possible, rather than getting drawn into secondary discussions.

√   Give them a job which allows them to be social but to complete a project, e.g. class surveys, joining the school council as a rep, encourage them to find a creative side - video reporting etc. If the issue they are avoiding might be writing, give different ways to show understanding and check it.

√   Avoid confrontations with the class clown, feeding their need to be the centre of attention. Recognise that clowning around often hides low self-esteem and anxiety about the work. Try to get their actual level (for example, of literacy) assessed or check with your SENCO, because this is often hidden. Give them a job which uses their talents, e.g. make up a funny song/joke based on the keywords or learning in this unit.

7 THE OMNIPOTENT PUPIL

'I need to be in control'

This child needs to keep control of their environment and the people in it by acting as if they are all-powerful and that they do not need anyone. Unlike the hypervigilant child (above), who sees danger in the environment and seeks safety from the teacher, the omnipotent child will often have experienced dangerous, unreliable or rejecting adults, and will avoid them. It can sometimes mean that a child has had to be an 'adult' way beyond their years, and to act as if they have everything under control outside school. In class you will see it as the pupil who acts as if they know everything already and better than the teacher. They can't ask for help: they don't follow instructions and insist on doing things their own way. They may attempt to exert control over the class and bully others into feeling powerless: they may seem arrogant.

As we saw earlier (p.17), omnipotence is a defence we use when we feel threatened, powerless or not in control. It can happen when a child has had a sudden loss or trauma in their early years or when the child generally feels powerless in their life outside school.

NEEDS

These pupils' basic need is to keep control and to hide their wounded self, to protect them from humiliation and pain. Taransaud (2011) describes this kind of omnipotent self as an internal rescuer, which keeps the wounded self hidden from shame. They act as if they want to be feared and admired, but underneath it are often fearful. For any learning to take place, the student needs to feel that they are protected from humiliation and pain. They need:

▷ to ensure they don't feel powerless and that unexpected catastrophes can't happen to them again. To feel they have choices and are in control of them

▷ safety and security to be in their hands: they view the world as a place full of potential danger. But, unlike the hypervigilant child, who will often seek proximity and support from the teacher, the omnipotent child can't trust the adults to keep her safe. Also in contrast to the hypervigilant child, a child showing this kind of pattern can settle to do a task independently until she needs help with it from an adult (but won't ask).

▷ To feel they have choices and are in control of those choices

▷ A nurturing adult who understands the vulnerable, hidden part of them. The danger is that omnipotent behaviour often provokes the adult into acting omnipotently as well, meeting the child's need to control with a desire to prove the adult is more powerful.

STRATEGIES

√ Develop activities which allow recognition and acceptance of powerful feelings and allow the student to defeat the teacher through learning, e.g. competitive games such as hangman or battleships teach children how to win and lose safely.

√ Use creative activities and metaphor to help pupils explore feelings in a safe, 'contained' way, e.g. stories, drawings, modelling, games, videos, soaps. Comment in the third person, in an indirect way, on stories and TV which allow all feelings, e.g *Where the Wild Things Are* (Sendak, 1963).

√ Make use of films and stories with good/bad in one character, e.g. The Hulk and Superhero/villain, Spiderman, so that the pupil can learn about integration: that everyone has different parts to their personality.

√ Allow choice and control: don't find yourself being drawn into unnecessary power struggles, and pick your battles. Avoid trying to exert power and control when it is not needed because you will miss opportunities to give the student the choices they need.

√ See the wounded child behind the omnipotent behaviour and relate to him/her.

8 THE PERFECTIONIST PUPIL

'I can't bear to get it wrong or to upset the teacher'

Not all children with attachment difficulties act out in class or come to our attention as a concern. The perfectionist child attempts to stay under the radar, to do everything just right' and to not be a bother to the adults. In class this can be seen as:

- taking a long time to get ready for work, carefully choosing pens and paper
- finding it difficult to hand in finished work, particularly course work in secondary, because it is never 'good enough'
- drafting and re-drafting work
- continually rubbing out and starting again
- being compliant but sometimes erupting suddenly when things go wrong
- always saying everything is OK even if they seem quite subdued

NEEDS

These pupils may have learned to behave this way due to living in environments where they are unnecessarily punished for mistakes or where the adults are coping with such adversity and crises that the children get overlooked. They need:

▷ to have the anxiety recognised and named
▷ to learn to understand and bear the frustration of getting it wrong
▷ to learn to take safe risks and experience making mistakes in a safe environment
▷ to have some control over their work and their world

STRATEGIES

√ Instead of reassuring the pupil about being 'good-enough', name the anxiety about being not being perfect

'You cannot bear to get it wrong or less than perfect. It is possible for something to be good and also need some improvement.'

'Not knowing something can feel terrible.'

√ Acknowledge how hard it is for the child to change his beliefs about himself

'You find it hard to believe this is good enough.'

√ The skill these pupils need is to learn is to allow some imperfection or middle ground between perfect and useless. Use any opportunities to show that everyone makes mistakes and can learn from them. Wherever possible, include your own examples of learning through making mistakes. You also need to model this, so if you get something wrong, admit it or wonder with the class how to do something better.

'It's normal and OK to make mistakes.'

9 THE PUPIL WHO RUNS AWAY

'I need to be in control'

This type of child seems continually poised to flee the classroom and the learning situation. They may actually do this, creating great anxiety and concerns about health and safety, or might threaten to do so. In fact they often don't leave the school grounds but can be found in potentially dangerous places such as the school roof, or hidden in places such as cupboards or under the chairs.

NEEDS

▷ this child need to be safe and sometimes believes the way to be safe is not to be noticed, so may hide in the building. However, they might also be checking out if they will be remembered and their absence noticed, so they will run around the school building as well. Essentially they are in their 'flight' mode where people and things are dangerous.

▷ they need to know that the adults can keep them safe and that on a very basic level, the building is safe.

STRATEGIES

Above all try to contain your own anxiety and have a plan with other staff.

√ Try not to buy into the expectation that they will run out of your class at any opportunity but also show them that you can cope if they do: you may need to say directly that your job is to keep them safe.

√ Allow them to sit near a door if needed, or somewhere with a good view of the room; sometimes the need to escape is mitigated by knowing you can.

√ Talk to the SENCO and TA and make sure a plan is in place if the pupil does leave your class.

√ It's important not to show your panic. Let them know you are in charge, and you can keep them safe.

√ You can explain your concern for their safety and reassure them that you can keep them safe in here.

10 THE PUPIL WHO RUBBISHES THE WORK

'I am rubbish so anything I do is rubbish'

This student rubbishes their own work and any attempts to praise it. You might also see this type of behaviour from a student with an avoidant attachment pattern, who, when unable to make progress with their work without adult help, rips up or spoils that work rather than allowing the teacher to intervene. However, the avoidant student will not usually be interested in rubbishing other people's work or drawing your attention to their own failings.

The child with a disorganised attachment pattern who rubbishes work can also be quite negative about other students' work and your attempts to help them. This rubbishing shows up in class as:

- calling out negative remarks
- refusing to do work and saying it is pointless
- ripping up work that is nearly finished
- reacting badly to praise and refusing to publicly accept certificates
- seeming generally unhappy and unmotivated

NEEDS

There can be several reasons for this type of behaviour. For many students it is a sign that they feel that they are rubbish and 'bad'. They may fear humiliation and criticism, and will ward this off by being the first to criticise their work and the world around them.

▷ to have adults who recognise the anxiety behind the behaviour
▷ to learn how to bear disappointment and frustration at making mistakes
▷ to feel safe enough to accept some praise and to recognise their own strengths

STRATEGIES

√ For students who find it hard to accept that their work is finished and 'good enough' allow them to use mini-whiteboards to draft out work and to keep portfolios of work at different stages.

√ Avoid getting drawn into their negativity and have ways to change your own emotional state when you are feeling demotivated. This kind of projection often happens with these students.

√ Focus on their strengths, find different ways to give praise, talk for example about the task rather than praise the child.

√ Acknowledge any feelings: *'Maybe you find it hard to believe, but this is good.'*

√ Have activities which allow them to take out their frustration in different ways, e.g. battleship type games, jenga etc.

√ If the student generally seems unable to allow positivity about school, frame the activities in a less 'school-like' way, e.g. talk about projects rather than tasks, portfolios and events rather than school trips, team work rather than group work

11 THE PUPIL WHO CONTINUALLY LIES

'The truth is unbearable and you won't like me if I tell the truth'

The pupil who continually tells lies can be a great source of annoyance to many teachers. They are often seen as defiant and delinquent, with no understanding of moral values.

The student who lies or makes up improbable stories and keeps to the story in the face of it being disproved can make teachers and other students very confused and angry. We often put great value on 'telling the truth and owning up,' when in fact, lying should not be seen as an act of defiance, more like a cover-up of anxiety and as a learned behaviour.

NEEDS

We need to understand why students might lie, in order to better understand the needs that are driving them to behave in this way. These can be:

▷ to manage excessive stress. Lying can be both a result of excessive stress in a learning situation and a defence mechanism to protect from this stress.

▷ to provide escape from unbearable realities. Sometimes pupils lie because they create fantasies of how they would like to be or how they would like life to be, and sometimes they can convince themselves that the fantasy actually happened. This happens particularly if they are from abusive backgrounds, where lies and fantasy can be an escape, a way to manage trauma.

▷ to learn to use their working memory better. Sometimes they genuinely do not remember exactly what happened (see p.92 on memory).

▷ to manage 'down-time' and boredom. Sometimes pupils lie because they are bored. They make up more creative versions of events to create entertainment.

▷ to protect themselves from potential exposure to punishment or interventions from outside authorities. Sometimes it is a learned behaviour

- they may have learned not to tell people the truth about what is happening at home or to share information with anyone in authority.
▷ to shield themselves from shame. Some students can't respond honestly in situations where they have done something wrong because they experience intense feelings of shame. They attempt to protect themselves from these feelings of shame by lying, minimising the wrongdoing or their part in it or blaming others.

STRATEGIES

√ Stay calm. If a student continually lies about events, try to remain calm and not accuse them of lying. If the student refuses to accept responsibility in class, don't force it in the moment, talk to them afterwards when they are calm as well.

√ If your school asks you to pursue the matter, collate the information factually and present it to the student. State the facts and say that this is what you or other people saw and heard. Acknowledge that the student might have seen it differently. Say for example, *'I understand that you think that is what happened, however, X says …'*

√ Work through relationship, not blame. Be careful with too much focus on the behaviour. Recognise that shame underlies the behaviour, and don't spend too much time and attention on the lying: this will only increase feelings of shame and reinforce the need for the shield. Aim to make a connection and work with your relationship with the child before attempting to correct them. Shame can be regulated through showing empathy and understanding to a child who continually lies. In this way the child may learn to take responsibility for the behaviour, instead of being overwhelmed by the shame and the need to defend against it.

- √ Try to work out what makes this pupil anxious. Are there particular things that the pupil lies about, or to particular people? If you notice a pattern, can you help them to break it by finding other ways to deal with the underlying anxiety or belief?

- √ Make a future focus. Ask the pupil *'How can we make sure this doesn't happen again?'* This is far more effective than having an inquest and insisting on apologies.

- √ Use their imagination. Use the student's ability to lie in a creative task and to help them understand the difference between truth and lies. Ask students to re-write a comprehension passage and include at least three lies from the original. Younger students can simply change three words, for example, *John likes ice-cream* can become *John doesn't like ice-cream*. Other groups have to spot the lie.

Chapter 5

Difficult times

1 BEGINNINGS, TRANSITIONS AND ENDINGS

Routine, structure and consistency are vital for pupils with attachment difficulties. This means that there are times in the school year which can make these pupils very anxious, when those routines and structures are relaxed, change or even disappear. Essentially these are the times when there is something ending and new things beginning: transitions from one class to another and around the school, endings of terms, changes of teachers, transition from primary to secondary and so-called 'fun' days such as sports days and break times.

Unless you are involved pastorally with your pupils, you might not need to be overly involved in some of these transitions but there will be times when it's important to be aware of them and plan for them if you can in your lessons. For example, coming up to a break, some pupils will be anxious, may exhibit lack of focus and poor behaviour and may need as much structure as possible to be maintained. If you know you are going to be absent from school, or if you're actually leaving, you will need to have a plan with other staff, particularly the pastoral staff and teaching assistants to support any pupils with attachment difficulties.

Why times like these are difficult

Children and young people with attachment difficulties have often had many endings and transitions in their lives and these endings or transitions may have been sudden and disruptive - involving the loss of loved ones through bereavement, families splitting up, the continual movement of home, changes in parental relationships, or even imprisonment. So changes can feel unsafe and bring back feelings of anxiety and uncertainty.

These concerns don't always show up in the form of worried, anxious children, with whom we might easily empathise. Anxiety can show in clowning around, fighting and being aggressive, or even in physical illnesses.

WHAT CAN WE DO?
1   Transitions and Endings

Transitions and endings give us an opportunity as teachers to show these children another model of how to manage an ending. We can help them to understand that someone can go away, and still 'hold you in mind'. They can learn that you, the teacher, and they, the pupil, can hold onto the memories of what you have both learned and shared together. With their uncertainty and anxiety empathised with, reflected on and contained, they may also be able to learn how to start looking forward to the positives of moving on.

All the activities opposite are examples of marking an ending in the 'proper' way (*for more ideas about transitions and ending, see* Bombèr, 2011).

Be aware of your own feelings around endings. It can be difficult to let go of children with whom you have had a close working relationship and for whom you may still have anxiety about the future.

STRATEGIES

If we begin to see transitions in this way, we can easily develop some ideas for marking the ritual and learning from it. Some ideas I have found useful are:

√   Let children know in advance if someone is leaving and arrange a proper opportunity to mark the occasion. Marking a goodbye honours and respects the relationships developed.

√   If possible, work up until the last minute of term: children with attachment difficulties often cannot bear the uncertainty of lack of structure. If this isn't possible, have some mechanical structured activities for them to do even if they are off timetable.

√   Have a leaving party.

√   Mark the changing of relationships with other pupils as well. One nice way to do this is with a group writing activity where everyone writes their name on a paper and then passes the paper round for each pupil to write something they like or will remember about that person.

√   Have a final circle time to allow people to say what they are feeling.

√   Create a group photo or picture.

√   Don't take stuff down from the classroom walls when children are still around.

√   Get children to write letters to themselves or to new children. Write a letter yourself to the class.

√   Make a memory book - best moments in this class.

- √ Encourage a review of work: what we were like and what we have learned.

- √ Make use of stories: journeys are good ones to read or make up. A pupil can write a collaborative story about a journey which involves the idea of moving on.

- √ Make use of appropriate symbolic activities - tidying up, putting away, and sorting things out.

- √ Plan an ending in advance wherever possible. Be clear about dates and plan a proper event to mark the ending. Avoid the temptation not to tell them until the last minute. If you have had good classroom management, it will not disappear overnight.

- √ Allow time for pupils to mark their sadness at the ending and honour their relationships. They may express this as anger or rejection, but bear in mind this is a normal part of the loss process.

- √ Acknowledge your own feelings to them. If it is hard to leave, let them know. Don't be afraid of marking the moment and be aware that some of the feelings you are attributing to the group may indeed be your own.

- √ Have a tangible product for them and you to take away, such as a group photo or memory book.

- √ Spend some time on looking at the positives of transitions and changes.

- √ If possible, liaise with new staff, and arrange for them to meet their new teacher or find out information about the new school situation.

- √ If your class is moving on, get them to write letters to your next class about what to expect and what it's like in your class so that they can acknowledge their own learning and development.

2 Unstructured time

Unstructured time is also a minefield for children with attachment difficulties. As we have seen their greatest need is safety and consistency, so the parts of the day with less structure, such as breaks and lunchtimes, can cause great anxiety.

STRATEGIES

- √ Find out if your school has any structured clubs and activities at break and lunchtimes. If there are any, encourage the pupil to join a group they might enjoy or ask another child to suggest this. Accept that the pupil might sometimes need somewhere quiet to sit during breaks, or may need a job or something to do during a sports day.

- √ Try to have a plan with breaktime supervisors. These pupils can find it difficult to self-regulate during breaks and can become too rough, too excited, too angry, too stressed or too withdrawn at these times.

- √ Remember to think developmentally about breaktime tasks, and don't assume the activity needs to be age-related. Think about emotional age.

- √ If you can, encourage the pupil to take part in structured games together with at least one other child, but probably not in big group, because they need to learn how to socialise with others in a step-by-step way.

- √ Acknowledge and name any difficulty you see the pupil is having:

  'I have noticed that you find it difficult to manage in large groups at break, how about we think of a plan to help you with that ...'

- √ Set up a lunchtime buddy scheme in playground for all children. For example, some schools have a friendship bench where students can sit if they want someone to play with and other students can come and join them.

SUMMARY

▷ Transitions and endings can be very difficult times for children and young people who have experienced disruption and trauma. Such changes can evoke old feelings and remind them of losses and other often sudden, traumatic and unsatisfactory endings. It's important as a teacher to be aware of potentially difficulty transitions and endings and to plan accordingly. You can create an opportunity for children and young people to experience a more positive ending and to learn the skills to manage these.

▷ There will be other parts of the school day when pupils with attachment difficulties might find it hard to cope, particularly unstructured and less supervised times such as breaks. They will need help and some structure to manage these times.

Chapter 6

Difficulties with learning

COMMON PROBLEM AREAS

As a classroom teacher it can seem impossible and overwhelming at times to pay attention to every pupil's individual needs and life circumstances. Of course it is very important that we try to see all our pupils as individuals, and to understand the particular difficulties of pupils with extra needs, such as those with attachment difficulties. However, in reality, we often teach many classes and large numbers of pupils with a wide variety of needs. The good news is that any strategies which support the learning of pupils with attachment difficulties will also benefit other pupils in your class. It can be helpful to focus on the areas which most affect the learning of children with attachment difficulties and to develop teaching strategies which then address these areas for everyone else. There are four key areas:

1	**Working memory**	*which affects ability to pay attention, focus and follow instructions*
2	**Empathy**	*which affects relationships with staff and other pupils*
3	**Self-esteem**	*which affects motivation, mood and behaviour*
4	**Communication**	*which affects the ability to learn and work with others*

In this chapter I'll show how you can build in strategies and activities to address these issues, suitable for all your pupils.

1 PROBLEMS WITH WORKING MEMORY

Working memory is the part of the brain which allows us to hold information recently given to us and to act on it. For example, when you are told a telephone number and are trying to remember it while looking for a piece of paper to write it down, you are using your working memory.

Pupils with attachment difficulties often have problems with working memory because they are preoccupied with fears and anxieties about the class, learning and relationships. Their brains are on 'fight or flight', causing them to be hypervigilant and continually on the look-out for potential and imagined dangers, with no space for reflection. High levels of the stress hormone cortisol may have flooded their brain in their early years, impairing the growth and development of certain parts of the brain. Childhood trauma can lead to connections between the neurons not hooking up properly. They may not have learned to trust their own thinking capacity, and so don't expect to remember things.

Working memory is very important for pupils to help them learn well in class. Difficulties with working memory can lead to pupils:

- Not following instructions because they can't remember them
- Not remembering what they have just read, because they can't hold the information in their minds
- Not being able to keep their place in activities, for example, remembering which line they are reading in a text
- Having issues with problem-solving activities, where you have to remember the previous parts of the sequence to move onto the next
- Keeping focus in class and on track with work
- Having problems with general organisation, for example being in the right place at the right time with the right equipment

STRATEGIES TO HELP WITH POOR WORKING MEMORY

There are simple classroom management strategies which can help pupils with poor working memory. Many of these will be known to you, so you're already on the right track, and hopefully you'll also find some new ones to try out. They are all strategies which should help all your pupils, but vital for pupils who are struggling with working memory problems.

REMEMBERING AND FOLLOWING INSTRUCTIONS

It is important to pay particular attention to how you give instructions. Pupils with working memory problems can't remember long lists of instructions and will often need non-verbal reinforcement. You can help them by:

√   Giving instructions on a step-by-step need-to-know basis.

√   Avoiding long verbal lists of things to do: use gestures and pictures to make clear what you want.

√   Writing the instructions on the board and/or using visuals to show the order of upcoming activities. For example, use an icon of a book for the reading part of your lesson.

√   Giving an example of what pupils should do in an activity, and then ask for another example from the class before getting started.

√   Avoiding the use of sequencers where possible. For example, if you say 'Before you open your books, I want you to look at the board', the brain will hear 'Open your books,' and organise itself to follow that instruction. Instead, say - 'First I want you to look at the board'.

√   Wherever possible, give the action words last. This will be the word pupils will remember if they are not good listeners or finding it difficult to pay attention. For example, you might say: 'OK, I'll play the dialogue again, ready? Listen'.

RECORDING HOMEWORK AND REVISION

Copying from the board can be difficult for pupils with poor working memory because they can't remember what they have just read and can't hold it in mind long enough to write it down. This means that they often don't get homework written down or their key points for revision. Wherever possible, use handouts in class for key points, and technology such as apps for homework and revision.

DEVELOPING MEMORY

Pupils will need help and support in developing ways to remember important information. You can work with all your pupils on simple ways to aid their memory. Some ideas are:

- √ Mnemonics: these are simple memory devices which help pupils to remember the order of larger pieces of information, often in the form of a rhyme or humorous sentence. For example, a mnemonic for remembering the sequence of the colours of the rainbow is: Richard Of York Gave Battle In Vain (Red, Orange, Yellow, Green, Blue, Indigo, Violet).

   Some pupils might like to draw a picture which represents their mnemonic. For example, to reinforce the mnemonic for the colours of the rainbow, they might draw a knight, Richard of York, fighting and losing a multi-coloured battle. The visual can be another way of triggering memory.

- √ Organisation: pupils with working memory difficulties need help with organisation and keeping track of where they should be. They may benefit from having a visual timetable, where the lessons are represented by an icon or picture as well as the words. They will also benefit from visual checklists and memory prompters.

- √ Memory prompts: pupils also need structured prompts to trigger their memory and to remember important routines and instructions. This can take the form of questions to themselves which will prompt recall. They can be posters or bookmarks for the front of their books.

√   Memory posters: create posters for the wall (and if necessary for individual pupils) with key prompts to recalling instructions. For example:

> **MEMORY PROMPTER**
> What do I have to do first?
> What will I do next ?
> Who am I working with?

√   Stay patient! Expect to repeatedly remind pupils who have attachment difficulties about routines and timetables.

READING STRATEGIES

Poor working memory affects a pupil's ability to read and remember longer texts. This means that they find classroom activities which require reading comprehension difficult. They very quickly forget what they have just read and lose track of the information.

√   Wherever possible, use reading texts which can be given in short, 'do-able' chunks.

√   Include *learning to learn* strategies in your lessons, where you give all your pupils tips on how to improve their reading comprehension strategies. For example, encourage them to highlight the key words in a text, to notice the beginning and end of paragraphs where information is often summarised, and to become aware of their own self-talk and ways to use this as a memory and motivation tool.

ENCOURAGING POSITIVE SELF-TALK

Encourage pupils to notice when their mind has drifted and to bring it back. Let them know that it is normal for our minds to drift away sometimes, particularly in groups, but that we can begin to notice and then develop ways to bring it back.

√ Encourage them to pay attention, to develop some positive self-talk and to ask, 'How can I bring my brain back now?'

√ Or to stop and pause at regular intervals when reading, and ask, 'What do I already know about this?' and 'What have I just read?'

GIVE BRAIN 'DOWNTIME'

Pupils with attachment difficulties often feel that there is no more room in their brain for thinking about learning. Even apparently simple learning tasks can cause excessive anxiety, fear and frustration because, as we have seen, these pupils have not usually had support to manage the feelings aroused by learning in the classroom. This means that their brains often need a way of 'switching off' and resting. All your pupils will benefit from occasional brain 'downtime', but it is essential for pupils with attachment difficulties. Ways to do this include:

√ Having a drink of water.

√ Practising some mindful breathing, for example, breathe in for the count of 4 and out for the count of 7, and do this a few times.

√ Closing your eyes and daydreaming, giving the mind permission to wander.

√ Spending a couple of minutes doodling.

√ Listening to relaxing music or imagining listening to a favourite piece of music

HELP WITH SELF-REGULATION

Pupils with poor working memory often have problems with self-regulation and will blurt out answers and comments in class at inappropriate times. You can help them to manage this by, for example, using mini-whiteboards where pupils can hold up their answers instead of answering verbally, or by encouraging them to learn positive self-talk.

SUMMARY

DIFFICULTIES WITH WORKING MEMORY	STRATEGIES
Forgetting what to do	Memory bookmarks, posters
Not copying from board	Use handouts
Not remembering homework	Give it out on printed paper or through an internet forum rather than copying from the board
Not having right books/equipment	Check in at start of day Have spares
Losing place when reading	Use ruler/ tracker
Not understanding or remembering what just read	Underline, colour, self talk
Calling out all the time	Teach anchoring of states (*see p.148) Use mini whiteboards
Losing focus	Encourage them to notice when it happens and to 'bring their brain back'
Daydreaming	Take brain breaks Checklists of what to do

2 EMPATHY

Children and young people with attachment difficulties can find it difficult to empathise with others. This might be because they haven't yet reached a developmental stage where they can imagine what it is like to be another person. Also, if they haven't had the experience of being thought about in their early or current lives, they won't have learned to think about others. In addition, some children with attachment difficulties view the world as a very dangerous place and as a result often misread the intentions of others in a negative way. This makes empathy very difficult. This can cause problems with learning in class because:

- They find it difficult to predict the reactions of the teacher and the consequences of their own actions. They will sometimes continue to behave inappropriately despite being warned of or even having experienced the consequences.
- They find it difficult to work with their peers in pair and group work, sometimes taking over the task completely, jumping in when it is not their turn or not noticing when others are becoming annoyed with them
- They do not always notice when another pupil is upset or having a difficult time and may seem uncaring. This in turn can cause problems with their peers and the teacher who may view it as unkindness
- They find learning tasks difficult which involve imagining another person's point of view or understanding another person's life, for example, English and History, tasks which involve writing from the perspective of a character in a book or at a time in history (see p.132).

STRATEGIES FOR DEVELOPING EMPATHY

All pupils will benefit from activities which create empathy and understanding in your class. They help to build an inclusive ethos where pupils can feel accepted and a sense of belonging. We have seen in Chapter 3 that one way to do this is through your class rules about kindness and supporting others. Another way is to plan to include activities which encourage pupils to think about other people in the class and to include pupils who might not be in their usual friendship groups. For example:

MY SECRET FRIEND
All the class write their names on a piece of paper and give it to the teacher. The teacher puts all the names in a bag. The pupils pull out a name and do not show anyone. This is their 'secret friend' for the week. Each pupil must try to be nice and kind and friendly to this person without telling the secret friend. For older pupils, you can adapt this activity slightly to committing random acts of kindness. Explain that research has shown that we all feel more positive and happy when we do something kind for other people. We also feel positive when a stranger does something nice for us for no reason, even a small thing. Have pupils choose names from the hat and explain that they should try to find opportunities to do random acts of kindness for that person in the coming week.

GAMES
Games give pupils an opportunity to learn to share and think about others. Classroom games which involve predicting another person's strategy or response are particularly helpful for developing empathy skills.

- ✓ Don't give up if some of your pupils break the rules of the game or act in a silly manner. Children who haven't had an opportunity to play will need to practise the skills of playing. Getting it wrong is a learning opportunity. Stop the game and check the rules. Check everyone knows why we need rules - to make it fun and safe. Acknowledge the difficulty: *'It's hard to lose, no-one likes it: but let's try again.'*

√ 'I'll answer for you': Students work in groups of four. One student sits on a chair and two students stand behind her. The fourth student asks questions to the student on the chair. They should be questions about the student - their likes/dislikes, and so on. The student on the chair remains silent and the two standing behind have to answer the questions for her, trying to imagine what her answers would be. The student on the chair simply nods or shakes her head to indicate how accurate the answers are. The students take turns in the different positions.

√ This game is an excellent practice of the skill of empathy, 'walking in someone else's shoes'. It can also show students how they come across to others. The content of the questions can be changed to reflect topics being taught, but the basic skill of empathy is the main focus (it's important to put a few boundaries around the type of questions which can be asked). The activity can also be adapted to allow pupils to imagine the replies of a character from their English book, or from a history period they are studying.

(For other ways to use the curriculum to teach empathy, see Chapter 8).

SUMMARY

DIFFICULTIES ARISING FROM A LACK OF EMPATHY	DEVELOPING EMPATHY - STRATEGIES
Hurting other children physically or emotionally	Teach pupils to empathise by imagining how a character in a story or book would feel in a certain situation. Reinforce your class rules on staying safe and keeping others safe.
Not being able to play and share	Use games and be prepared for them to go wrong, use them as a learning experience.
Not being able to use words	Take every opportunity to name the feeling a pupil is having or that is shown in a story/text/film. Help pupils to extend their vocabulary for expressing feelings through games and activities.

3 SELF-ESTEEM

Pupils with attachment difficulties often develop low self-esteem with regard to learning and the classroom can become a very daunting place. This can occur for several reasons. They may have had an early experience of adults who humiliated or overly-criticised them for mistakes when learning to do something. This can lead them to re-experience extreme feelings of stupidity and worthlessness when they find a task difficult in class. If they have an ambivalent-resistant attachment pattern, they may not have separated out enough from the adult to trust their own thinking when trying to do tasks in class. This will mean that they easily feel helpless and believe they cannot succeed independently.

Some will not have had experiences of adults who could contain their feelings of anxiety and the fear of making mistakes, so they are reluctant to get things wrong. Children with attachment difficulties often view mistakes as proof that they are stupid, and will not take risks with learning for fear of humiliation and failure.

Children with attachment difficulties often feel 'different' to other children in the class, and this feeling of not knowing how to belong can lead to low self-esteem In class, low self-esteem can cause difficulties because:

- Pupils often give up very easily
- They may act helpless and don't trust themselves to work independently
- Pupils can easily become frustrated at tasks when they get stuck or make mistakes
- They are not easily reassured by praise and encouragement from the teacher because it does not fit with their poor self-image
- They will not take risks in learning and make little progress as a result

Take every opportunity to build self-esteem in your pupils and to encourage them to believe they can learn. Good self-esteem is essential for learning and taking risks.

STRATEGIES FOR DEVELOPING SELF-ESTEEM

BUILD ON STRENGTHS

At the many meetings around our pupils with difficulties, particularly those with behavioural problems, we often tend to focus on the problems and ways to solve them. We also need to spend time focusing on the pupil's strengths and interests. Pupils with poor self-esteem may believe that they're not good at anything. Try to notice and build on any skills which they do have, such as drawing or sports, or on other more personal qualities such as kindness and fairness. For example, if they are good at drawing, perhaps they can draw the posters for the classroom rules, or if they are good at noticing unfairness, give them the job of making sure everyone takes a turn in a game. In this way, they might also be practising something which they personally find difficult, such as turn-taking.

√ Don't label the pupil as lazy if they appear to be daydreaming or not answering in class. Often pupils with attachment difficulties are trying really hard and not making much apparent progress.

√ Celebrate mistakes as a way of learning by talking to pupils about how mistakes helps all of us learn.

PUPIL OF THE WEEK

Notice, praise and encourage other skills, particularly non-academic skills and personal qualities.

√ For example, give a reward such as a certificate for the pupil with good social skills, the pupil who is good at taking on responsibility, the pupil who perseveres and does not give up, the most empathetic pupil.

CREATING POSITIVE STATES FOR LEARNING

It is impossible to learn when we feel bad or stupid. Many pupils with attachment difficulties lose confidence before they even try a task or activity. They think they will be bad at it and so will have failed before they have started. You can teach pupils techniques for getting a positive feeling about learning.

√   **The confidence bracelet** (*This is an adaptation of an activity from NLP**) Ask students to think of a time they remembered something well. It can be quite a simple thing, such as always coming to class on time. Pupils might find it difficult to think of an example, so you might need to do this after you have played a game or done an activity where they showed you that they could remember something. Say to students,

'*See the time in your mind: hear what you were hearing, feel what you were feeling. Take the feeling and imagine I am turning it up, as we do with a radio or ipod: that's right, really feel the feeling*'.

Ask students to imagine a circle on the floor in front of them and, when they are ready, to step into it and take the feeling with them. When they are in the circle, tell them to feel the feeling in their whole body and to choose a word to say to themselves to remember this feeling. Then tell them to step out of the circle and imagine it can be picked up and put on their wrist as a bracelet. They should do this and put the bracelet on their wrist by encircling one wrist with their finger and thumb. Tell students that this 'confidence bracelet' is on their wrists now and when they want to remember something, before trying to do so, they should hold their wrist, say the word and the bring the feeling back. This will seem crazy to some students, but it works! (Delaney, 2016, p.125).

EEYORE AND TIGGER THINKING

Use characters from books or games which represent optimistic and pessimistic thinking. Many children with attachment difficulties have a pessimistic, catastrophic view of the world and their ability to learn. The characters of Eeyore and Tigger, for

DIFFICULTIES WITH LEARNING

example, from Winnie the Pooh, represent two different ways of thinking. Tigger is happy and optimistic. If Tigger gets five out of ten for his work, he thinks 'That's good, I know half of it, who can help me learn the bit I don't know?' and he probably gets six or seven the next time. Eeyore is very pessimistic and when he gets five out of ten he thinks 'You see, I told you I couldn't do it, I'm stupid, what's the point? I might as well give up.' And the next time he gets fewer marks.

√ This activity can be adapted for older pupils by asking them to pick or design the characters. Use it as a question in class - *'Is that a Tigger or Eeyore thought?'* - and begin to give children a new way of thinking about learning.

SUMMARY

DIFFICULTIES ARISING FROM LOW SELF-ESTEEM	STRATEGIES
Giving up easily	Teach optimistic/solution-focussed thinking
Overreacting to any perceived criticism	Focus on strengths
Not being able to accept praise	Give praise in different ways. Acknowledge in words how difficult it can be to hear good things when we are not used to it.

*NLP is Neuro-Linguistic Programming, a model of communication developed in the 1970's by Richard Bandler and Michael Grinder, based on analysing what excellent communicators seem to have in common, what they believe about themselves and others, how they behave and the precise language patterns they use. For further information see McDermott & O'Connor 1996. For applications to teaching, see Terry & Churches 2008).

4 COMMUNICATION

Many pupils with attachment difficulties also have difficulties with spoken and/or written communication. This can be because the part of their brain connected to executive function has been affected. Executive function can be thought of as the way in which the brain 'circuitry' organises and controls some of our abilities and behaviours. These connections within the 'HQ' of the brain particularly affect self-regulation and control of emotions. Children with poor executive function find it difficult to know when to speak, how to express emotions appropriately and how to organise their thoughts in a coherent way.

Children with an *avoidant attachment pattern*, who do not trust relationships with adults, will often not have developed the skills of verbal communication which usually build up through relationships with caring adults. In addition, children with high anxiety, and who are preoccupied with thoughts of other dangers in the learning environment, will often find it difficult to stay in the 'here and now' for long enough to pay attention and answer questions appropriately in class.

Such difficulties can affect their learning and their relationships with other pupils in their class. Communication difficulties will show up more in classes where listening and speaking have a high priority. Pupils with communication difficulties may have problems in all classes with:

- Expressing opinions/thoughts
- Showing understanding
- Understanding and following instructions
- Interaction with peers

STRATEGIES TO HELP DEVELOP COMMUNICATION

EXPRESSING OPINIONS
Pupils will often need time and help if they are asked to speak in any class. The use of thinking time, pair work and small group work can help these pupils greatly.

√ Think, Pair, Share: When pupils have to respond to a question or give an answer to the teacher, give them time to first think of their response on their own, then ask them to discuss with a partner and then ask the pair to tell the whole class their answer. Wait or think time is very important for pupils with communication difficulties. They need time and rehearsal to formulate their thoughts.

SHOWING UNDERSTANDING
√ Use mini-whiteboards so that pupils can hold up their answers and don't need to speak in front of the whole class. Pupils write their answers on their own mini-whiteboard and have the chance to correct their ideas by rubbing out any answer they are not happy with (*for more ideas, see Delaney 2016, pp.28-29*).

RELATIONSHIPS WITH OTHER PUPILS
Pupils with attachment difficulties often have problems in their relationships and communication with other pupils. Sometimes they are unable to express their feelings and wishes with appropriate language and can appear rude, insensitive or domineering. They sometimes, for example, insult other pupils in an attempt to make a connection with them. Sometimes they use language in a way which other pupils find strange, for example, making random, silly remarks at inappropriate times. Some insecurely attached pupils never speak, and other pupils lose patience with them.

√ It is vital as their teacher to notice when this is happening, and to encourage all pupils to work together in different groupings and pairings throughout the year.

√ Pair work is particularly important as large groups can be overwhelming for pupils with communication difficulties, and they need practice in a small way first, gradually building up.

√ Study buddies: Encourage pupils to be kind to each other and to help each other. Implement a system of study buddies, where pupils can volunteer to help pupils who are finding certain things difficult. Set this up by emphasising that everyone has different strengths and difficulties and that by working together we can become better at things. Often pupils who are loud and get into trouble because of their behaviour can be good study buddies with a pupil who is quieter. It can help to sit the pupil with pupils who can speak up and who will help them to express their answers, but be careful to explain to the louder pupil that they have been chosen because they can be helpful. If you notice they are taking over the interaction, be prepared to change the pairings.

√ Alternatively, it can sometimes help to pair quiet children with each other, as eventually one of them will need to speak! Children with a secure attachment pattern can also be helpful if paired with a child with an insecure attachment pattern.

PAUSE FOR THOUGHT

Do you use any of these techniques already in your class? Can you choose one of the techniques that might be new to you, to try with your class?

SUMMARY

DIFFICULTIES ARISING FROM COMMUNICATION PROBLEMS	STRATEGIES
Needing time to think/not being able to speak up in a group	Use *Think, Pair, Share* to give thinking time Have a clear system about who should speak e.g. talking pen
Not expressing opinions/needs	Use buddy systems Have non-verbal ways to show feelings e.g. red card when time out needed
Not showing understanding/not understanding	Use non-verbal means e.g. mini-whiteboards, ABCD cards, smiley face cards Reinforce with non-verbal cues e.g. pictures/gestures
Not having right books/equipment	Check in at start of day Have spares
Not understanding and following instructions	Give and get example of what is needed Sit next to helpful peer Use prompt cards
Not understanding non-literal language	Be precise in your own use of language, specify who, what, when, where
Interacting with peers	Use activities which encourage working together, initially with a helpful peer e.g. shadowing, doubling, buddies

Chapter 7

The importance of teacher language

Language has huge conscious and unconscious effects on our brains and on our actions. By working on the precise language you use in the classroom, you can manage classroom behaviour positively, model effective communication, focus on working together inclusively and help children to give names to their feelings and emotions.

Pupils with attachment difficulties are particularly sensitive to teacher language because they will have learned through experience to pay close attention to adult words and behaviour in order to keep safe. They will often respond to the tone and meaning of a teacher's words in ways that a younger child might. So it's useful to pay attention to the words you use and the way you say things in the classroom, and to recognise that both hold the potential to create positive change if you use them well.

Thoughtful use of language can also help a pupil with attachment difficulties because it can present another chance for them to experience being thought about by a caring adult. The psychoanalyst Bion commented (1962) that *we learn to think by being thought about*: one way we can show children that we are thinking about them is through our use of language. For example, we can try to notice what they are feeling and if appropriate, name that feeling for them.

> I'm wondering if you're feeling discouraged right now?

> I'm wondering if that made you feel really proud, you look like you feel really good?

The key therefore to working with children with attachment and behavioural difficulties is to use language which keeps them safe, shows that you understand their anxieties, and gives them clear boundaries: but, at the same time, also creates a positive expectation *of* them with regard to learning and behaviour.

LANGUAGE FOR CLASSROOM MANAGEMENT
Focusing on learning

When thinking about the language of classroom management, it's important to remember that above all we want pupils to come to school and learn. This may seem obvious, but often we only talk to pupils who are having problems with behaviour about their behaviour. The language we use often emphasises *what kind* of behaviour required, and doesn't explain *why* this behaviour is important: *'Sit still, focus on your own work, stop calling out,'* and so on.

It's important that we try to keep the focus on the learning. Otherwise, such pupils become disengaged from the main reason for school, and their learning potential becomes blocked.

Class rules/contracts

So, when setting rules for behaviour and classroom rules, establish an ethos with your language which is inclusive, and keeps the focus on safety and learning.

For example, at the beginning of a class, when setting class rules, you can ask,

THE IMPORTANCE OF TEACHER LANGUAGE 113

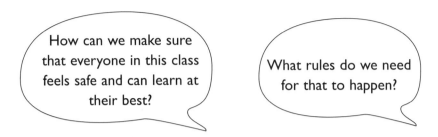

If you set these type of rules, when pupil are having problems with their behaviour and becoming disruptive, you can draw their attention to the *effect on the learning climate* by saying,

> Learning isn't taking place now: so how can we change this situation?

A real advantage of this approach is that it takes away any moral judgment about anyone being singled out as 'bad' if they're not 'behaving properly' - it makes the comment more neutral, matter-of-fact and collaborative. And it is after all reminding all of us why we are all there - to participate in and enjoy learning.

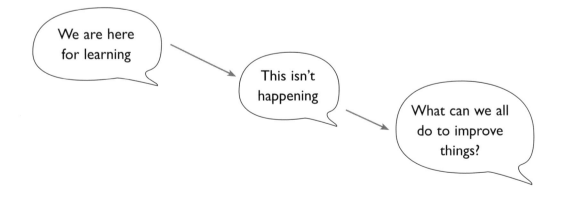

Think about the values you want to promote in your class. As we have seen, children with attachment difficulties need safety in relationships and need to learn trust and empathy for others. All pupils will benefit from learning these values and your classroom will be a more peaceful, co-operative place if you spend some time on this and use this kind of approach. Draw up class contracts with your class which focus on the values you want in your class. Here are some examples:

- We speak kindly to each other
- We allow people more thinking time if they need it
- We use our words to solve problems
- We listen to other people in a respectful way
- We help others when we can

When reminding pupils of the class rules, make sure you remind of the underlying *values*:

Remember we don't speak to each other like that in this class

What's the rule in this class about listening and not laughing at others?

Dealing with conflict and verbal challenge

We have seen that some pupils will constantly engage the teacher in arguments and conflict. For some these will be learned patterns of interaction, may be examples of *transference* (*see* p.15) or defences learned at a young age, or of avoiding the frustration of not feeling good enough or shame at not being able to do the work.

Breaking the pattern and showing another way of behaving is essential with these pupils and not always easy to do in stressful situations. Learning and practicing some language patterns can help you to remain calm and assertive in the most challenging situations.

Show the pupil you have listened to what they are saying

Remember that listening to a pupil is not the same as agreeing with them. Also think about your listening skills - are you *listening to understand* or *listening to reply*? Very often, particularly when we feel under stress, we don't listen to everything a pupil is saying to us because half-way through we are thinking about how best to reply. This can prevent us from understanding the real issue the pupil is having or struggling with.

Listen to the whole communication and show the pupil that you have heard and tried to understand what they have said. You can acknowledge their feelings and objections by reflecting back what they have said, or naming the feeling you observe in them.

> I understand that you think this is unfair and I can see that you are angry

Using *and* rather than *but* allows the pupil's brain to hear both parts of the statement. When we hear *but*, our brain tends to only focus on the negative part of a sentence.

When you have *acknowledged* what you hear and see, you can still be assertive and state your boundary or sanction.

> ... and I need you to stay behind to finish this work

It's essential that we understand and acknowledge that a pupil might have different needs and behaviour outside the class. Remember that many of these pupils will have learned behaviours which keep them safe outside school. These behaviours may not be appropriate in your class, such as constantly shouting and arguing loudly. You can show with your language that you acknowledge their basic need by saying,

> ... you don't need to do that/be like that in here

By saying *in here* you're letting the pupil know that you understand they might need to behave differently in another environment. By using the word *need*, you're acknowledging that their behaviour was developed in response to a genuine need they might have had, and is not just a way of causing trouble for you.

State the safety

As we have seen in previous chapters, safety is the most important need for children who have lived in unsafe, volatile and inconsistent environments. Above all, emphasise the safety in your class and your ability to keep your pupils safe emotionally and physically. For some children it's necessary to state this explicitly by saying, for example,

> It's safe in this class. It's my job to keep everyone in this class safe

Avoid shaming

Be careful not to induce shame which is often easily felt by children with attachment difficulties. These children may have been in environments where they were shamed and humiliated. Overly negative comments don't teach these children 'how to behave': they often induce feelings of shame and self-loathing, which can lead to demotivation and further poor behaviour. This is unhelpful to all children, but particularly damaging to children with attachment difficulties who have often been rejected, discouraged and mistreated by adults at some stage in their life.

Unhelpful negative language

"I have told you that you cannot do that in here" — *does not explain what they should do*

"You are disrupting this class and stopping others from learning" — *singles out and shames*

"Stop being so rude, you are always so rude" — *creates negative expectation and relationship*

"It's not unfair, everyone has to follow the same rules, you are no different" — *for those who understand the world literally, such a comment invites examples of this not being true*

Giving instructions

As we have seen in previous chapters, pupils with attachment difficulties have problems remembering what the teacher has just said, which affects their ability to follow instructions. Use positive, specific language to support pupils with this. Tell pupils what you *want them to do*, rather than what you *don't* want them to do:

If you say the second comment, a lot of children will automatically turn around. Our brains process the action word before the negative command and if our brains are pre-occupied and on high-alert, finding it hard to focus, they will definitely follow the action word. If possible, praise those who are doing what you want rather than criticise those who aren't:

Be as specific as possible. For example, *'Joe, pass me the blue pencil on your table, thanks.'* rather than *'Joe, can you pass me the pencil?'* If Joe has comprehension difficulties, he may become anxious and wonder *'Which pencil?'* With some children this can result in blocking and freezing, and with others there might be a more volatile reaction such as throwing all the equipment on the floor. Not what you were hoping for out of nowhere on a Thursday afternoon!

Dealing with disruptive behaviour

When disciplining, use language to state the behaviour you want to see and to show that you have a higher expectation of the pupil. Wherever possible, describe what was inappropriate and indicate an example of the appropriate behaviour. You might say, for example, to a child who has been rude or unkind to another pupil,

> I know you are a kind person. That was unkind today, when you would not let Mary join in your group.

By holding up a positive expectation, we try not to further hurt the wounded child

> I saw you being kind when you asked Mary to sit next to you. I want to see more of that …

> You are funny. You can be funny without hurting other people …

LANGUAGE FOR HELPING PUPILS TO DEVELOP EMOTIONAL AND SOCIAL SKILLS

Notice and name the skills they need to practise

During the class, notice and acknowledge things which are going well. Give specific praise. General praise such as *'You are being good today'* doesn't teach children what the appropriate behaviour is. Instead, say something which highlights the observable behaviour: *'Well done for being patient and waiting your turn.'* Always be polite, however tempting it is to say something sharp or sarcastic. These children need to have the appropriate way of speaking modelled by the teacher at all times.

Constantly model what you want with verbal and non-verbal behaviour.

It is important to notice when the child who often gets into trouble is showing the appropriate behaviour, even if this means noticing what they are *not* doing! For example, you might say to a child who has been continually interrupting in previous lessons - *'Thank you for listening without interrupting'*. Most children who behave badly at school say that they are no longer noticed when they start behaving appropriately. Noticing good behaviour and commenting on it teaches them that they can also get acknowledged for doing the right thing.

If you have recognised that the pupil needs to develop skills such as trusting others, accepting help, trusting their own thinking, try to notice when this is happening and give specific, positive feedback on it.

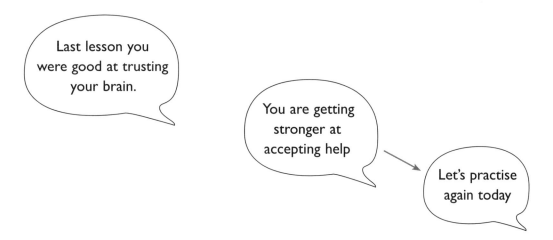

Name and normalise feelings

Children with attachment difficulties often have powerful feelings which they believe are wrong and make them bad. It's important wherever possible to name any feelings you notice and normalise them. Some teachers are worried that this will open a Pandora's box or make the pupil more emotional, but this isn't the case. When we feel understood, we all tend to calm down and are able to think better.

Saying to an angry child *'I can see you are very angry and upset now'* won't make them more angry. It's an example of *containment* (*see* p.50).

Learning to translate behaviour

Children with attachment difficulties often have problems understanding the effects and consequences of inappropriate behaviour. They may find it hard to generalise norms and rules from one context to another. In order to learn how to behave appropriately, we need support from an adult who can 'translate' what their behaviour might mean and what the behaviour of others means (Bombèr 2007). One way to do this is to separate out descriptions of behaviour from how it can be interpreted, or how it might feel for that person.

Simply telling a child to stop doing something is not teaching them why and giving them an alternative. It's vital that children who have not learned these things in their early years, learn them in class. So describe what you see, and separate this out from what you feel or your interpretation, and give the positive instruction of what needs to happen:

Similarly, telling a child to *'Calm down'* or *'Be patient'* is too general and vague for children with attachment difficulties. They often haven't had any experience of calm environments or patient people, and may have no experience of what it feels like to be calm or patient. Even words such as 'kind' may be meaningless in reality to a child who has not had much kindness in their lives.

So you can describe how the inappropriate behaviour might make people feel: then describe a kind behaviour, and explain how that might make someone feel.

If possible, give the child a strategy to help them to do the thing you are talking about: for example, being calmer.

Or remind them of a reference experience:

Emotional scaffolding

Schofield & Beek (2006) describe how children who have experienced trauma and loss need 'supportive scaffolding'. As a teacher, you will know about the *scaffolding of learning tasks*, giving pupils enough support to gradually be able to do the task alone. Some pupils also need *emotional scaffolding*, where the teacher notices what is happening, describes it and helps the pupil to manage the feeling. For example, you can say to a child who is getting very restless and losing focus:

THE IMPORTANCE OF TEACHER LANGUAGE

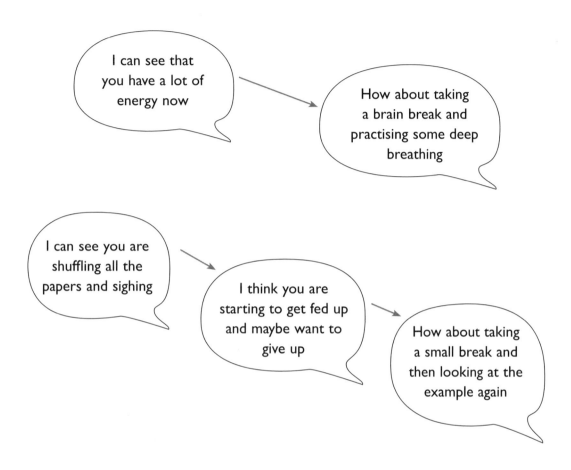

Another form of this is 'wondering aloud' - similar to the reverie identified by Bion in which a caregiver responds to the baby's crying by wondering aloud what it might mean (*and see* p.22): '*Are you tired, hungry, frightened by that loud noise?*' You might notice what a child is doing and help them to connect to what it might mean, by using the phrase '*I wonder...?*' or '*I'm wondering ...?*' You don't need to know what the behaviour means. The important point of this strategy is to try to understand and wonder with the pupil what it might mean to them.

> I notice that when you are getting anxious, you start to rock on your chair

> I wonder how we can help you with that

> I notice that you sometimes …

PAUSE FOR THOUGHT

What language have you found effective in class?
Do you use any of these strategies already in your class?
Can you choose one of the strategies that might be new to you, to try with your class?

SUMMARY

The language used by the teacher has a powerful effect on pupils. Many pupils with attachment difficulties have not had an experience of an adult who has helped them to understand the world and relationships by naming what is happening for them.

The language used by you as their teacher can give them a second chance to experience this and to develop a more positive self-image as a capable learner. Ways in which you can do this include:

▷ Keeping the focus on learning and the learning climate.

▷ Using your class rules and contracts to involve your pupils in developing an inclusive learning atmosphere and linking these rules to the values you want in your class.

▷ Practising really listening to your pupils and reflecting back what you are seeing and hearing. Where appropriate, name and normalise their feelings.

▷ Using calm, assertive language when dealing with conflict and keeping the focus on what needs to happen rather than dwelling on the problem. Direct attention to the present and future rather than past regressions.

▷ Using language which shows you recognise the need beneath a behaviour and explicitly stating that need wherever possible, particularly when related to safety.

▷ Helping the pupil to understand the meaning of their own behaviour by using language to 'translate' what might be going on for them, based on what you observe and wonder about it.

▷ Noticing and naming social and emotional skills being developed and used.

Above all, it's essential to understand the powerful impact of your language and to practise using it in a positive, descriptive way rather than a negative, judgemental way. Children with attachment difficulties have already had too much negative, harmful language in their lives.

Instead of ... *(negative and blaming)*	**Try...** *(positive and assertive)*
Your behaviour in the last lesson was terrible. Any more of that and you will be on report.	Let's have a great lesson today, I know you can do it.
Hurry up and clear up this mess. Your table is always the last and the messiest.	OK, which table can be first to clear up and be ready to go? Yes, well done that table at the front, who else is ready?
Stop disrupting the class and interfering with other people's learning, I'm sick of telling you not to do that.	Jack, get on with your own work, thank you. You have only 5 minutes left to finish it. If you need help, please ask me.
Don't be so rude, you upset everyone with your rudeness.	I know you are a kind person and want to see you practising being kind today to everyone.
Stop this awful noise, everyone in the other classes can hear you.	Thank you to those sitting quietly. I will wait for everyone else.
Don't run down the corridor, it's dangerous and silly.	Please walk down the corridor. It's safer for everyone.
If you don't stop messing around and finish that work, you won't be allowed to take part in the football match after school. You'll be in detention.	OK, how can you get that work done and make sure you'll get to your match in time?

Chapter 8

The curriculum as a vehicle - challenges and opportunities

You will have been trained to plan your lessons according to subject content, and to differentiate the work for students of different levels. It can also be helpful to think about the *effects of the actual curriculum* on some children with attachment difficulties, and consider how to differentiate for them.

The underlying concepts of certain subjects can provide challenges and threats to these pupils. However, they can also provide us as teachers with the opportunity to work with some of their anxieties, and to support them to develop skills they did not acquire in their early years.

I am not suggesting that you need to develop a whole new set of resources. But you need to be aware of the possible challenges and opportunities in your curriculum. You can then adapt known activities to meet some of these challenges.

THE CHALLENGES AND OPPORTUNITIES
1 The content of a lesson
The *actual content* of some subjects can be worrying for children with attachment difficulties. For example, topics in PHSE such as '*Me and my family*' can be difficult for children in care or for those who have fragmented families. For secondary students, modules in English and Foreign Languages which require talking about

yourself and your family present similar challenges. It is vital to be aware of these potential issues and give other alternatives.

However, less obviously, the *underlying concepts* in some subjects can also provoke conscious and unconscious anxieties and memories in some children.

HISTORY

History can be scary for children with disrupted and confusing backgrounds. For example, some pupils may have moved several times in their lives and cannot keep track of the number of places they lived or the times and dates of key events in their lives. They find it equally hard to bear the thought of thinking back in time, because the past may involve a lot of bad memories. The simple act of drawing up a timeline for events in a period in history can seem overwhelming. They may act as if they cannot understand the concept at all. At some level, these children and young people may find it safer to stay in the 'here and now' than to allow their brains to accept the concept of past time.

✓ Be aware that apparent resistance to learning can be because it involves looking back. If appropriate, you can name this and say, 'Some people don't like to look back in time, they prefer the future, and that's OK.'

✓ Give them another alternative if possible: for example, create a character such as a time traveller who is back in the past and noticing the differences. Looking at the world from the point of view of a third person provides safety for children who have experienced trauma in their own lives.

OPPORTUNITIES
★ History also offers pupils the opportunities to think about the world from different perspectives, to develop empathy and to explore the different motivations of historical figures.

GEOGRAPHY

Some aspects of Geography relate to people and places. For children who have no fixed place or do not know where they belong, the study of populations, towns and countries where people have a sense of identity and connectedness can seem unimaginable. They may consciously reject the subject by saying it is boring and pointless, or unconsciously by seeming not to be able to learn. Geography may stir up unwanted questions about where they come from, or stir up feelings of loss, disconnectedness and pain at the displacement of loved ones.

- ✓ Be aware that students who say the topic is boring or that you are a boring teacher might be having problems with the concepts being studied.

- ✓ Include discussions and examples of populations where migration and change regularly occur, and opportunities to discuss the inherent challenges.

OPPORTUNITIES
- ★ Geography also offers opportunities to explore different countries, places and cultures, and to consider how identity and belonging is created.

ENGLISH

We often ask children to write about themselves or their personal experiences in English. Sometimes they are required to write an autobiography or curriculum vitae. This can be extremely painful for some of our pupils, as it involves reflecting on their lives and life events. They often disrupt the class and do not complete tasks, but are unable to explain why. Again their objections to the work (boring, pointless etc) may not be the real reasons. For others, it is impossible to write about themselves because they have no sense of self. Structuring stories can also be problematic for children whose minds are chaotic.

- ✓ Be aware that a student who is refusing to write an assignment in English might be finding it too personal. If possible, give them options about how to do the assignment differently. For example, allow them to invent a character or change the information.

- ✓ Acknowledge their feelings, *'Maybe you don't like to write personal information, that's OK.'* Show them the marking criteria so that they can understand they will not be marked on how much personal information they divulge. Explain to them who will be reading their work. They may be worried about exposing their story to a wider audience.

- ✓ If a pupil does write a harrowing personal story, be careful how you respond. If you only mark the story for content and grammar, for example, you will be dismissing their experience. The story might feel overwhelming to you and you will need some time to process your feelings. Remember you do not have to fix their lives, just show that you have read and understood what they have written.

- ✓ Acknowledge this: *'Thank you for sharing your story with me. A lot of difficult stuff has happened already in your life.'* Of course if they disclose information that suggests there might be a child protection issue, or that the pupil might need some extra support, you will need to consult your senior manager about this.

OPPORTUNITIES

★ Stories, plays and drama in English can provide a natural vehicle and sufficient psychological distance for children and young people to explore their feelings in a safe way.

SCIENCE

Some elements of the Science curriculum involve ordering, sorting and classifying items. It can be very hard to understand the concept of logic and order if you have not had much or any of this in your life experience. Children who seem to understand many Science concepts cognitively can sometimes seem perplexed by activities which involve classification.

✓ If students need help with sorting and categorising, allow them to work with a helpful classmate. Give as much practice as possible, for example, with games and matching activities. Students may need an element of overlearning with these concepts.

OPPORTUNITIES

★ Science also offers the opportunity to practise ordering, categorising and understanding the need to persevere to find things out and to learn that each 'failure' actually contains useful pointers to the next step needed. Pupils who find it hard to take risks and make mistakes in learning can be reassured by examples from Science, where great discoveries have been made by 'failing' and trying again.

MATHS

For some children, Maths can be a strange subject. It involves thinking about whole things, parts of wholes, adding up, taking away and general accepting the idea of splitting being OK. For those who have fragmented, complex, confusing family relationships, there can be an unconscious resistance to the idea of breaking things up, adding and taking away 'for no reason'. For others, the idea of adding and subtracting can be dangerous as there have been so many examples of loss and complexity in their relationships.

On the other hand, for other pupils, Maths can seem safe. Right and wrong is clear. There is a structure and a process which leads to a right or wrong answer. The world seems clear and unambiguous, and this may provide comfort in an otherwise upsettingly uncertain world. Maths offers opportunities to explore patterns, sequences, divide up and put back together, put some order into the world.

- ✓ Understanding or confusion and anxiety about wholes, adding and splitting may be worth bearing in mind with a child who seems unable to apply the basic concepts. It can be helpful to simply say something like: *'I know it can be hard to understand that in maths you can take away and replace things, whereas in life you cannot.'*

OPPORTUNITIES

- ★ Maths does give the opportunity to work on problems which have a clear, logical structure and definitive answer. For younger pupils, there are rarely any 'grey' areas with Maths: this can be quite soothing in their otherwise 'messy' world, providing a degree of order. For older pupils, learning a step-by-step way to solve equations and complex mathematical operations can help them to develop problem-solving and logical thinking skills. They can practise breaking tasks down into 'do-able' chunks and learn not to be overwhelmed by the apparent size of a problem.

OTHER STRATEGIES ACROSS THE CURRICULUM

You can also see your curriculum as an opportunity to explore ideas with all pupils which will help them emotionally and developmentally, and which will particularly help the pupils described in this book. It is possible to choose activities which meet the needs of pupils with attachment difficulties identified earlier, for example connecting up, sorting out, expressing feelings safely, developing empathy, putting order into chaos. The types of activities which can help include:

- ✓ Jigsaws can be created to revise the content for most subjects, and have therapeutic value for pupils who have lives where things are pulled apart and not put back together.

- ✓ Matching activities where pupils match words and pictures, questions and answers, with the concepts on cards or to be joined up with a line all have a value for pupils who have suffered loss and need to make connections.

- ✓ Finding differences, finding people and things in a picture are all helpful therapeutically for children who are feeling lost.

- ✓ Put it in a frame: A simple way to contain anxiety is to draw a frame around any worksheets you are using. Somehow this makes it safer than the empty page.

2 Themes to explore

POLAR OPPOSITES

Children with attachment difficulties often have problems understanding the middle ground. They tend to be 'all or nothing' thinkers, which makes learning very difficult when they feel confused and not sure. This is because they have not always passed through the stages known as *constancy* and *permanency*, when children learn that a caregiver can be angry with them and still love them.

The curriculum offers opportunities for students to explore the idea of polar opposites. In subjects such as English and History, for example, you can explore how a hero can exist without a villain: whether any character or person is really all bad or all good: what motivations might people have for their behaviour. In History, you can consider the perspectives of different historians on famous people.

In PE you can discuss the different facets of some sports stars. For example, they can seem arrogant as players, and yet give millions to charities in their countries - so, are they are good or bad people?

DIFFICULTIES FACED AND OVERCOME

Another theme which can be helpful is that of *working through difficulties*. Again this can be discussed through characters from history, in Geography by tracing migration and development, in Science through experiments and inventors.

DEVELOPING EMPATHY

As discussed in Chapter 3 and on p.98, children with attachment difficulties often have problems empathising with other people. The curriculum offers many opportunities to discuss empathy and what it would be like to be another person. For example, living in a certain period in history with a certain status or job, understanding the customs and cultures of other countries, understanding the motivations and personalities of characters in a novel, famous scientists and their reasons for persevering, famous people and what it would be like to be them.

Part of developing empathy is to understand different perspectives. On a practical note, certain subjects involve viewing objects from different views and dimensions, for example Art, IT, Graphic Design, and exploring different issues, Drama, English and History. Children with attachment difficulties sometimes have very fixed views on the world and activities: encouraging them to try seeing things from different perspectives can help them to become more flexible.

PROBLEM-SOLVING AND CONFLICT RESOLUTION

There are many opportunities in the curriculum to practise problem-solving and conflict resolution in a safe way. In History the origins of conflicts and disputes can be discussed and evaluated, and explored further in English and Drama. Step-by-step problem-solving can also be practised in Science and Maths.

JOURNEYS

The metaphor of a journey, with many trials and tribulations, can be very engaging for children who have faced difficult times, even in a short life. Any opportunities to write and read about journeys should be exploited, for example, in History, Geography, English and in PE, the sporting journeys of stars.

SUMMARY

▷ The curriculum offers challenges and opportunities for working with children with attachment difficulties. Certain subjects might stir up difficult feelings and memories both consciously and unconsciously. Subjects can provide space to work on important issues in a more indirect, less threatening way.

▷ So as teachers we can choose activities which have a dual purpose: to teach the subject, but also teach a social or emotional skill which pupils need to develop and may not have learned in their early years.

Chapter 9

Managing your wellbeing

WHY YOUR WELLBEING IS IMPORTANT

It is vital that you look after yourself so that you can deal with the challenges of teaching vulnerable children. Teaching is about nurturing relationships, and it is very difficult to do that when you are not in the best emotional state yourself. One of the major factors on pupil behaviour is the reaction of the teacher. *Our* physical and emotional states affect learning and teaching, as much as that of our pupils'. So being able to manage yourself, your feelings and your reactions is an essential part of teaching. It is not selfish to pay attention to your emotional and physical state, to be aware of your own limits, energy levels and resourcefulness - it's crucial.

Most of us thrive on a certain level of pressure. But if that tips over into us feeling drained, then it can be dangerous and eventually lead to burnout. That's why teachers often get sick in the school holidays. If you have been working on high levels of adrenaline and stress, often ignoring the symptoms of not coping, when you have a chance to relax your body lets you know what was happening was too extreme. So let's think about wellbeing and highlight strategies for caring for ourselves better. Wellbeing can be considered in three ways:

- **mental and emotional wellbeing**
- **physical wellbeing**
- **social wellbeing**

> **PAUSE FOR THOUGHT**
>
> What do you do to maintain your wellbeing in these three areas?
> What about when you are busy and stretched at work?
> Do you prioritise your wellbeing or does it come at the bottom of your to-do list?
> Remember, it's impossible to do a good job of caring for others if you do not look after yourself.

Dealing with stress

There is a lot of talk nowadays about the increased demands and higher stress levels in life in general. Teacher stress in particular has been the subject of much debate and discussion. So before we look at how to improve wellbeing, we need to consider the issue of stress.

How would you define stress? It can be useful to consider the amount of pressure which we can cope with to enable us to work at an effective performance level. Many of us are not that motivated by too little pressure, or staying in our comfort zones. There is usually an optimal amount of pressure in response to which we perform well. This could be the type of pressure which puts some demands on us but in a way that increases our performance. Williams (1994) calls this optimal amount of stress being in the 'stretch zone'.

So stress is not always related to increased pressure of workload. The danger is that we are not always aware when the demands of work have tipped us from the 'stretch zone' to a 'strain zone' where we are continuing to work hard but for less results. Most of us have indicators which tell us we are overstretching ourselves and going into this danger zone for stress or strain. For example, perhaps you start to get aches and pains in your muscles, upset stomach or headaches: or you find it harder to make decisions, take longer to do simple tasks, are more irritable and prone to emotional outbursts. We often do not pay enough attention to these indicators and begin to feel 'stressed'.

Sometimes we have a lot of things to do and we don't feel stressed, we feel energised. This is probably because we are doing things which we like and which use our strengths. On other days we may have one or two things to do, and we feel really stressed. The two things are probably tasks that we are unsure of, which do not require us to use our strengths, or actually require a level of skill or capacity we don't have. So it is important to realise that our stress levels are not always connected to *how many* things we have to do.

> **PAUSE FOR THOUGHT**
>
> *What are the things that energise and drain you?*
> *What lets you know you are tipping into the strain zone?*
> *What helps you to move back into a more healthy zone?*

Of course it is important to recognise when there is a real imbalance between your workload and demands on you and your ability as a human being to cope. Being realistic about the amount of work you can take on, and how much of your to-do list is actually important, matters, as does knowing when to ask for help and support.

However, a lot of stress in schools is caused by the unexpected, the disruption we had not planned for. It is important to realise that this is normal, and that it is rare to have a day when nothing unexpected happens. As teachers we work with people, not robots. Reframing our attitude to these unexpected things can reframe our perception of it as stress.

Recent research by health psychologist Kelly McGonigal (2015, *The Upside of Stress*) focuses also on the importance played by *our attitude to stress*. We can sometimes get stressed about feeling stressed! It is important to be able to notice that we are too stressed and to want to do something about it. However, it can also help to realise that a certain amount of stress has a part to play in all our lives as a motivator and can help us to direct our energy into getting things done. There are certain times in a school year when this type of stress will almost inevitably rise - around the end of a long term, or in the build-up to exam season. McGonigal's research suggests that a stress response can be an indicator of your body rising to the challenge. Her research also shows that the body's built-in mechanism for resilience to stress is to release the hormone oxytocin. This makes you crave connection and social support. It acts on your body and your brain to protect you from stress. By becoming aware of this, you will see that connecting with others, asking for and offering support actually biologically affects your stress levels. Ignoring the effects of stress and saying *'I'm OK'* is not healthy. It will often show up in your interactions with challenging students. But working on ways to manage stress in a healthy way should make life a good deal easier. As McGonigal says,

> When you choose to view your stress response as helpful, you create the biology of courage. And when you choose to connect with others under stress, you can create resilience. Now I wouldn't necessarily ask for more stressful experiences in my life, but this science has given me a whole new appreciation for stress.   Kelly McGonigal, TEDtalk 2013

Mindfulness

You might find the practice of mindfulness a useful tool for managing your wellbeing. Mindfulness means bringing your attention in a deliberate and non-judgemental way to what is happening in the present moment. It involves taking a pause and allowing yourself to be in the moment rather than looking back on past mistakes or worrying about future events. It allows you to view your own actions and that of others with compassion and acceptance. This might mean that you notice that at times things are actually overwhelming and that it is impossible to get through your 'to-do' list today - and that's OK.

It can also be helpful to practise the action of 'savouring,' which means appreciating the positive aspects of the moment rather than focusing on the negative. Another practice associated with mindfulness is that of 'gratitude', which means taking a moment to acknowledge what you *have* in your life that you are grateful for rather than dwelling on what you *don't have* (*for more on mindfulness see* Williams & Penman 2011 *and* mindfulnessinschools.org).

PAUSE FOR THOUGHT

How does this knowledge affect your thinking on your stress?
Who can you connect with in times of stress?

STRATEGIES FOR IMPROVING OUR WELLBEING

PLANNING YOUR TIME
Drainers and energisers

Think about what and who drains you, and what or who energises you. For example, if you believe that talking to colleagues energises and supports your wellbeing, notice which colleagues have that effect for you. Sitting in the staffroom complaining about the school and certain children may feel cathartic on occasion, but over time can lead to a downward spiral of despair and be de-motivating. Be aware of the effect other people are having on your own state. Consciously seek out people who give you a positive energy.

Similarly, some activities will energise you and some will drain you. Usually we are energised by activities which use our strengths and interests and drained by those which we find pointless or don't feel like us.

Try to spend time in your day and in your week with the people who energise you and doing the things which you love, which also energise you and use your strengths. If you are having a particularly bad day or week, you might realise that you have spent a lot of time with 'drainers' and need to re-energise.

- ✓ Take a break: It can sometimes help to go away and do something completely different if you are trying to plan a lesson, for example, and it's not working out. Don't be afraid to abandon your lesson plan sometimes for part of your lesson if you and the students need a break. Teach the pupils, not the plan.

- ✓ Learn to say 'no': It can be very hard as a new teacher to manage your workload and demands on your time, but taking on too much will make you less effective in your main duties. Learn when you need to say 'No' to things, and keep a focus on what your main activities need to be.

- ✓ Nurture your relationships: Build and maintain positive relationships - with students as well as colleagues and friends. Any relationships you build with students in non-crisis times will help you through any more conflictual times. As identified above, the hormone oxytocin is created through connection and support of others. This hormone has been identified as a key protective factor in promoting resilience.

✓ Play to your strengths: Use your strengths to overcome difficult situations and join in things which make the most of your skills and abilities. Too many of us dwell on our weaknesses and forget to use our strengths.

MANAGE YOUR PHYSICAL AND EMOTIONAL STATE
Physical health
Don't forget about your physical health. Remember to try to eat well, take some exercise, get enough sleep and relaxation.

Acknowledge and manage your own feelings and behaviour patterns
✓ Teachers have feelings too. You are not a robot. Suppressing feelings will usually make you very tired and ready to explode in some way at a later date - whether with an emotional outburst or sickness.

✓ Take time if necessary to acknowledge to yourself the feelings you might be having after a particular difficult class or encounter with a student. It might help to realise that not all the feelings come from you (see p.6 *and* p.151). Some of them may be projections from your more vulnerable students, giving you some useful information about how they might be feeling.

TRIGGERS
Learn to know the triggers which alert you when you are becoming overwhelmed by work ,and know how to deal with them. As discussed above, some amount of stress is usually good for performance. It takes many of us out of our comfort zone and into a stretch zone, where we are working at a high level. However, it is all too easy to tip over from the stretch zone to the strain zone, where the pressure becomes too much for us.

✓ So notice when you are tipping into the strain zone and be aware of any triggers which will let you know this is happening. For some of us, this will be physical signs such as aching bones, upset stomachs and headaches, for others it is forgetting things, becoming more irritable, more easily moved to tears.

✓ What are your physical and behavioural signs? What can you do when you notice them starting up?

ANCHORS*
Be aware of what are known in Neuro-Linguistic Programming as anchors - positive and negative. These are things which we see, hear, feel, touch or taste which can recall a positive or negative feeling. For some of us it will be a picture of loved ones or a wonderful holiday. For others, it will be the sound of a voice. We can utilise these anchors to bring us back into a good state. For others it will be more immediate and practical: such as going into the cupboard and screaming! Other people know they need to take a few moments for themselves. Other people use music, playing certain tracks on the way to work to get them in the right mood. When we become conscious of the need to manage our state, we can find ways to do so.

USE MENTAL STRATEGIES CONSCIOUSLY
Use the STOP technique
Consciously use techniques which allow you to stop and take a step back from stressful situations. Try the STOP technique.

S = *Stop and take a step back*
T = *Take a few deep breaths - 5 in and 5 out*
O = *Observe - what is **actually** happening, rather than **what you think** is happening. This gives perspective*
P = *Proceed with something helpful - you always have a choice. What's the smallest thing that you can do in this situation that will make a difference?*

mindful.org/stressing-out-stop/

CULTIVATE POSITIVE SELF-TALK

When we get stressed we often get caught up in a cycle of negative, unhelpful thought patterns, and it's useful if we can catch this. Some of these patterns include:

- Jumping to conclusions, mindreading the intentions of others
- Predicting that things will turn out badly
- Dwelling on the negatives and ignoring the positives
- All-or-nothing thinking: viewing things as *'either ... or'*
- Interpreting what we *think* something means, rather than *noticing what is actually* happening
- Generalising from one or two events
- Deleting evidence to the contrary to prove yourself right
- Personalisation and blame: blaming self and others

Try instead to catch these thoughts as they happen, and to ask yourself: 'What would be a more helpful thought or another way of looking at this?' Ways to do this include:

✓ Noticing what is happening rather than rushing to judge what is happening.

✓ Focusing on what is within your control.

✓ Reframing someone's behaviour with a positive intention (*see below*). Find evidence to a contrary, more constructive view.

✓ Focus on what is working, what is positive - six things each day (*see below*).

✓ Acknowledge what you are feeling is OK: pay attention to it.

✓ Be your own best friend/coach (*see below*).

✓ Ask, '*How can we do this?*' rather than '*Why isn't it working?*'.

REFRAME - THE THINGS WE CAN CHANGE AND THINGS WE CANNOT
We usually spend a lot of time worrying about things over which we actually have no control. We can't predict that a colleague will be stuck in traffic, and we will have to cover. We can't predict that a child's grandparent will die suddenly. Make a list of the triggers, worries, anxieties you have. Sort them into two - those you have control over and those you do not. If you do, decide what to do, if you don't, put them into another compartment in your mind. Notice what are real problems and what are perceived problems (Delaney 2009, p.166).

FOCUS ON WHAT IS WORKING - SIX HIGHLIGHTS OF EACH DAY
As teachers we tend to dwell on those pupils we could not teach, those classes which did not go well, those parents who complained. Whilst it's useful to learn from mistakes, too much of this can be emotionally unhealthy and affect us negatively. At the end of each day, write down your six highlights - things that went well, pupils who learned, pupil who behaved, laughs you had in the staffroom: anything can be used (ibid, p.166).

It might seem forced and strange at first. Our brains might not be used to such positivity, but by asking ourselves 'What is working well?', we will cope better with the stressful situations. We will be in a resourceful state for thinking about the stressful situations and remember why we want to be teachers! Steps with these children will usually be small but we need to pay attention to that progress (ibid, p.165).

GIVING YOURSELF THE ADVICE YOU'D GIVE YOUR BEST FRIEND.
If you find yourself despairing and thinking you must be hopeless because you cannot teach a certain child, take a moment and think what advice you would give your best friend in this situation. You probably would not berate and de-motivate them by saying they should give up teaching! And yet, we often have an internal voice which does just that to us. Take the advice you would give someone else. It will usually put you in a better frame of mind.

ALLOW YOURSELF NOT TO BE PERFECT

As I mentioned in Chapter 1, there seems to be one driving force for teachers across the world - the desire to get it 'right'. This is, of course, commendable. However, when dealing with people and relationships, especially those children who are the topic of this book, there is no 100% formula, no way to get it 'right' all the time, because quite simply we are all only human. In his description of how infants develop emotional security, Winnicott talks about 'good-enough' mothering (Winnicott 1971). Trying to be perfect can have the opposite effect, because then we try to do everything for our pupils: we can either become too controlling or get too frustrated when we can't find an instant 'solution'. Part of learning is learning to bear the frustration of not knowing, or learning through feedback on mistakes. We need to remember this for ourselves.

REMEMBER IT IS NOT MEANT FOR YOU

We are often told in training that we should not take things personally. This is easy to say but sometimes feels very different in practice. I have found it more helpful to think of it in Gerda Hanko's terms of 'It is not meant for you' (Hanko, 1999, and see above p.6). In other words, these children and young people behave in the ways they do for all sorts of reasons, and the adults in a school are often simply the recipients of unconscious fears, anxieties and angry feelings from elsewhere. This can be an example of displacement (Box 5, see below).

4 MAKE CONNECTIONS

WHO ELSE CAN HELP?

- ✓ Make a list of who can help you and with what. If someone seems very good at dealing with challenging students, ask if you can observe their lesson or talk to them about their approach. Do not be afraid to learn from others.

- ✓ Work collaboratively with the parents/carers of your pupils with difficulties. Sometimes we can find ourselves in conflict with these parents/carers if we

BOX 5 DISPLACEMENT

This happens when an emotion we are feeling about a particular relationship or person in our life cannot be safely expressed toward that person, but is displaced onto another person or into another situation. We all do it at times. For example, think about a time when something has happened at work which has made you very angry and how you reacted that night at home to a relatively minor comment from your family!

Children with attachment difficulties will often have difficult feelings towards key adults in their lives which they cannot safely express with that adult. For example, a child who has witnessed domestic violence may well have very mixed emotions about their parents. They might be sorry for the victim, usually the mother, but might also be very angry at her for allowing the violence to take place. Equally, they will feel angry at their own feelings of helplessness in the situation and be ashamed of their unwanted feelings towards their mother.

These complex feelings are often displaced onto a strong attachment figure, most likely a teacher in class. It is safer to shout and rage at your favourite teacher than to show these overwhelming feelings at home. As the teacher, it can be helpful to understand that the pupil who seems to be personally attacking you may be doing so because you are a safe, containing adult who can understand and manage these powerful feelings in a way which another adult in their life might not be able to.

are only meeting to discuss problems. Invite them in to also share ideas about *what works* and what they can help with.

✓ If you choose to talk to a colleague, be clear what you want from them. There is nothing worse than unsolicited advice. If you would like someone to just listen to you, make this clear. If you want advice, ask for it. Avoid those toxic groups of negative people.

✓ Research from the field of positive psychology shows that people who connect with others and support others build up their own resilience and levels of positivity (Dutton & Heaphy 2003, Layard 2011, Seligman 2011).

✓ Make sure you are not becoming isolated. Under stress we often retreat from the world and our social circles, particularly if we feel we do not have time to be sociable. But as we saw above, connection is a key factor in wellbeing.

SUMMARY

▷ A certain amount of stress in teaching is inevitable. It is important to recognise when our stress response is becoming too great and to do something about it. Connecting up with others can negate some of the effects of stress. However, the greater issue of teacher wellbeing needs constant attention. It is important to consciously develop and use mental and physical strategies to maintain your own wellbeing. Teacher wellbeing directly impacts on the ability to manage challenging students and situations.

▷ And of course, you can share all these ideas with your students - they need to learn how to manage their wellbeing as well, in order to create healthy classrooms where they can have fun and learn.

APPENDIX A

OBSERVATION

Developing a pupil profile based on attachment *This template can be used to record observations of a pupil who may have attachment difficulties. It might be helpful for you to complete this over time, and to use it as a discussion document with other staff to help you develop teaching strategies for the pupil.*

PUPIL PROFILE : TEMPLATE

NAME OF PUPIL	
CURRENT LEVEL OF ATTAINMENT	
PRESENTATION IN SCHOOL	
General approach to school/classroom e.g. attitude, behaviour, progress	
THE LEARNING TRIANGLE	
Relationship	
Relationship/response to the teacher: e.g. able to ask for help, rejects help, engages with the teacher in a positive or negative way	
in the whole class group	
in a one-to-one interaction	
relationship with other staff inside and outside the class	
Task	
Approach and response to the learning task set by the teacher: e.g. attempts it independently, does not attempt without help, starts and finishes	
Approach to overcoming difficulties: e.g. what does s/he do when stuck or not sure what to do?	

Copyright Worth Publishing ©2017 *This form may be reproduced, by kind permission of the publisher*

RELATIONSHIPS WITH PEERS	
in the class group	
supervised	
unsupervised	
on a one-to-one basis or small group	
supervised	
unsupervised	

PLAY	
What stage of play has the pupil reached?	
Any other characteristics/ observations: e.g. response to changes to routine?	

UNCONSCIOUS DEFENCE MECHANISMS/PATTERNS	
What kinds of feelings have you observed in:	
the pupil	
yourself in relation to the pupil	
other people working with the pupil	
What kind of patterns of interaction have you observed between:	
the pupil and yourself	
the pupil and other staff	
the pupil and other pupils	

FURTHER INFORMATION	
e.g. background, home situation, triggers, things that calm the pupil	

Developed from the work of Heather Geddes, Caspari Foundation

Copyright Worth Publishing ©2017 This form may be reproduced, by kind permission of the publisher

APPENDIX B

ATTACHMENT CHECKLISTS

These checklists are designed to help you to observe the possible attachment patterns of any pupil you are concerned about. They are not intended to lead to a diagnosis or to the labelling of a pupil. If you notice that a child or young person exhibits many of the traits of one of the attachment categories, you should discuss your observations further with your line manager and SENCO.

THE PUPIL WITH AN AMBIVALENT-RESISTANT ATTACHMENT PATTERN

CLASSROOM BEHAVIOURS	OBSERVED?	Often …	Sometimes …	Never …
Finds it hard to focus on task for a reasonable period of time				
Continually engaging with the teacher for help or for discussion				
Impulsive				
Restless: sometimes emotional outbursts at teacher				
Often looking to spend time with teacher at breaks				
Can appear very sensitive, easily upset				
Teacher can feel like never doing enough to meet the needs				

Copyright Worth Publishing ©2017 This form may be reproduced, by kind permission of the publisher

CLASSROOM BEHAVIOURS	OBSERVED?	Often …	Sometimes …	Never …
Can seem overly clingy				
Teachers can feel manipulated				
Sometimes talks excessively or is the class clown to maintain adult attention				
Very focused on feelings				
Poor understanding of cause and effect				
Can escalate confrontation to hold the attention of others				
Oversensitive to perceived signs of rejection				
Finds it hard to maintain relationships and can appear possessive				

Copyright Worth Publishing ©2017 This form may be reproduced, by kind permission of the publisher

THE PUPIL WITH THE AVOIDANT ATTACHMENT PATTERN

OBSERVED BEHAVIOURS	OBSERVED?	Often…	Sometimes…	Never…
Refuses help from teacher or TA				
Can seem quite preoccupied and lost in a task				
Finds it difficult to accept praise				
Rips ups work and attacks the task when not able to do it				
Can seem very self-contained, good				
Can seem very absorbed in a task and doesn't like interruption				
Does not take risks				
Prefers closed tasks to open ended				
Seems indifferent to hurt				
Can seem withdrawn,				

Copyright Worth Publishing ©2017 This form may be reproduced, by kind permission of the publisher

CLASSROOM BEHAVIOURS	OBSERVED?	Often …	Sometimes …	Never …
Underachieving				
Limited use of creativity and imagination				
Likes knowledge based subjects, not feelings based				
Can seem self-reliant and independent				
Reluctant to ask adults for help				
More focused on activities than people				
Can appear solitary and isolated				
Fear of failure so no risks				
Seems indifferent to new situations				

Copyright Worth Publishing ©2017 This form may be reproduced, by kind permission of the publisher

THE PUPIL WITH A DISORGANISED ATTACHMENT PATTERN

OBSERVED BEHAVIOURS	OBSERVED?	Often…	Sometimes…	Never…
Unpredictable responses, can change from very quiet, 'switched off' to loud, agitated and aggressive very quickly				
Controlling within peer relationship, everything on their terms				
Immature in making friendships				
Acts like knows everything already, omnipotent				
Provokes, bullies or challenges others to keep feeling in control				
Anxious in new situations				
Can't cope with sudden changes				
Appears compliant but resists any attempts to be helped				
Hypervigilant, cant focus on a task				
Fight or flight easily activated				

Copyright Worth Publishing ©2017 This form may be reproduced, by kind permission of the publisher

CLASSROOM BEHAVIOURS	OBSERVED?	Often...	Sometimes...	Never...
Underachieving				
Struggles in less supervised settings such as breaks				
Show little empathy or understanding of feelings				
Can take things very literally				
Gets very frustrated and show this with extreme behaviour such as banging head against the wall				
Runs around uncontrollably				
Runs out of class unexpectedly				
Explodes into temper for no apparent reason				
Can be very abusive to the other children in the class				
Can be very abusive to the teacher, rubbishing their attempts to teach				

Copyright Worth Publishing ©2017 This form may be reproduced, by kind permission of the publisher

APPENDIX C

CPD (1) DEVELOPING YOUR SKILLS

It is important to keep developing your skills for teaching children and young people with attachment difficulties. One way to do this is to choose an area to focus on and consciously try to include it in your teaching. This checklist can be used to guide your thinking. You might also want to use it as useful evidence for your Teaching Standard Portfolio - particularly in relation to:

Standard 5: *Adapt teaching to respond to the strengths and needs of all pupils.*
Standard 7: *Manage behaviour effectively to ensure a good and safe learning environment*

SKILL	HOW I TRIED THIS OUT EVIDENCE/ACTIVITY	IMPACT ON TEACHING/ LEARNING/PUPILS
Think consciously about what underlying defence mechanisms might be in operation		
Recognise what might be coming from you, and what could be coming from the child		
Practise thinking about the child in terms of attachment styles		
Practise noticing what is happening with all your senses, and describing not judging		

Copyright Worth Publishing ©2017 This form may be reproduced, by kind permission of the publisher

SKILL	HOW I TRIED THIS OUT EVIDENCE/ACTIVITY	IMPACT ON TEACHING/ LEARNING/PUPILS
Re-frame behaviour and ask what underlying need it might be showing you		
Practise noticing patterns and breaking the expected pattern of response		
Get precise and curious about language. Use it to be specific about social and emotional skills		
Create a positive expectation of these pupils		
Wonder aloud and provide commentaries, both to individual pupils and the whole class		
Develop active listening skills which do not involve searching for solutions and suggestions. Take the time to listen to the whole communication		

Copyright Worth Publishing ©2017 This form may be reproduced, by kind permission of the publisher

SKILL	HOW I TRIED THIS OUT EVIDENCE/ACTIVITY	IMPACT ON TEACHING/ LEARNING/PUPILS
Expand your planning skills to plan tasks which take into account the student's emotional and social development needs, and attachment needs		
Include left-brain tasks as differentiation for calming down if needed		
Include games which allow pupils to develop play skills		
Work with metaphor and creativity such as stories, drama, art		
Manage your own state for teaching. Develop conscious strategies to get into the right state and out of unproductive states		
Learn as much as you can about other people who can help. Arrange to meet with them regularly, rather than only reactively when there is a crisis		

Copyright Worth Publishing ©2017 This form may be reproduced, by kind permission of the publisher

SKILL	HOW I TRIED THIS OUT EVIDENCE/ACTIVITY	IMPACT ON TEACHING/ LEARNING/PUPILS
Remember that parents/carers will have the same anxieties and issues around the behaviour of the child. Strive to understand this, and avoid a blaming approach		
Find people who are good at teaching pupils with attachment difficulties and learn from them. Find out their beliefs about these children and notice how they react towards them. Also notice how they respond to critical incidents		
Pay attention to your own and others' health and wellbeing		

Copyright Worth Publishing ©2017 This form may be reproduced, by kind permission of the publisher

APPENDIX D
CPD (2) APPLYING YOUR LEARNING - CASE STUDIES

These case studies provide an opportunity to apply the thinking framework in this book to some realistic examples from the classroom.

You can work through these case studies on your own or with a group of colleagues. In each example, read through the description of the student and think about the questions underneath. When you have thought about/discussed the questions, move onto the next page and read the 'additional information'. Then think about/discuss the next set of questions. When you have done this, read through them and compare to your own thoughts.

Although some suggested answers are included in the final part of the case study, there is not a definitive right or wrong answer in any of them. They are included to help you to further develop your own skills in thinking about attachment and to guide you through the conceptual process.

APPENDICES

Case study 1 — Julie's anxiety

Julie is a 12-year-old, year 8, pupil who is driving her teachers to distraction. She came to her secondary school from a small primary school where the staff were able to give her a lot of individual time and attention. She enjoyed this attention and seemed to be happy in primary. She has not been assessed as having any specific learning difficulties but she has been allocated some support from a teaching assistant. because she finds it so difficult to focus on her own work and to get tasks finished.

Despite getting this special help, Julie continually seeks more attention from the teacher during lessons. At the beginning of a lesson she usually jumps up out of her seat when the teacher enters the room, offering to give out the books and write the date on the board. She insists on doing these things even when other pupils have been assigned to the task and gets very upset if she is not allowed to help.

During the lesson she constantly interrupts the teacher, sighing loudly, saying she does not understand what to do, not starting her work unless the teacher is standing next to her and continually demanding extra help. When the teacher or the teaching assistant come over to help her, she often tries to engage them in social conversation rather than asking them about the work.

If she is not acknowledged immediately by the adults, she gets angry and sulky, shouts at the teacher or runs out of the room saying that no-one cares about her. She spends so much time trying to attract individual attention from the teacher that she rarely finishes work and is often in detention for non-completion of homework. She seems to enjoy staying behind in detention. She spends most of break and lunchtimes outside the staffroom door, insisting that she needs to talk to her form tutor or head of year.

Her form tutor says: 'I find Julie's constant demands for my time and attention very draining. It seems like nothing I do is good enough. She always wants more. I often find myself snapping at her and then feeling guilty, because I also feel sorry for her.'

A space for reflection

- ⇨ What is your immediate reaction to this account of Julie and her behaviour?
- ⇨ What extra information would you like to know?
- ⇨ What underlying defence mechanisms might be in operation?
- ⇨ What might be the attachment pattern?
- ⇨ What needs might Julie be trying to fulfill?
- ⇨ How could her actions be re-framed with a positive intention?
- ⇨ What needs to happen to help Julie maintain a focus on learning and teaching?

Some extra information

Julie has been in and out of foster care most of her life. Her mother has a history of drug and alcohol addiction. Her mother has made several attempts to kick the addictions and as a result at times has been allowed to care for Julie again. On these occasions she has shown that she is able to provide safe, consistent care for Julie. However, despite this, on repeated occasions, Julie has had to been taken into emergency foster care as her mother has not managed to stay clean from addiction and relapsed drastically.

During her early years, Julie moved school several times due to her numerous foster placements.

A space for further reflection
- What do you think now?
- What pattern of behaviour does Julie expect from adults?
- What are you now thinking about her anxieties, defences and attachment pattern?
- What are her needs and how can these be met in the classroom and by the school itself ?
- What emotional and mental state would it be important to maintain as her teacher ?
- What strategies might work for Julie?

What is happening for Julie?

Julie appears to be exhibiting an insecure/ambivalent-resistant attachment pattern. She cannot focus on the task because she is too worried about maintaining the relationship with teachers.

Julie has learned that you cannot trust the mood of adults and that you need to be hyper-vigilant in monitoring the relationship you have with them. She cannot believe that when an adult leaves you, they can still think about you and 'hold you in mind'. She has not had any experience with this.

Neither has Julie had any experience of a secure base from which to explore the world. So she needs to stay close to the teachers, perceives other young people as competing for the scarce resource of the teacher's attention, and cannot take her attention away from the relationship for long enough to do the task.

Julie needs to develop the required separation from the adult in order to learn and concentrate on the task. She needs some amount of reassurance that this is safe to do, and that the adult will still be available as a secure base if help is needed. She needs the teachers to show her that she is being held in mind (by them) when they are absent, but to learn that it is OK to separate long enough to do the task.

Teaching strategies, therefore, should be designed to meet the needs demonstrated by this attachment-seeking behaviour. The temptation with these children is to give them the complete attention they appear to demand. It is important to understand that in the long-term, this is not helping the child or young person develop the required separation for learning to take place.

PRACTICAL STRATEGIES WHICH MIGHT HELP

- ✓ Try to ensure that you do not collude with the pupil's behaviour by giving the continual attention she seems to demand. Find ways to 'break the pattern', whilst emphathising with the need behind it.

- ✓ Reframe the discussions around Julie to answer the question *'What are her underlying anxieties and therefore her needs?'* Her main anxiety is that the adults might forget her when not with her. So find ways to let her know this is not the case. For example, mention something you remember she said in the last lesson.

- ✓ Develop a consistent set of strategies in every lesson which allow you to acknowledge her in class without distracting from the task. For example, give specific time limits for activities, and use a tick-list, where you can tick at regular intervals that Julie was on task.

- ✓ Build in ways through which Julie can get some individual attention, but make it a constant, regular time rather than 'on-demand'. For example, allow her to help one lunchtime to check lunch tickets.

- ✓ Help Julie develop other relationships with peers, for example, by asking older peer mentors to meet up with her in specific lunchtime clubs or by working on a project with others in her class.

- ✓ Wherever possible, name Julie's feelings when she seems anxious and attention-needy. For example, you might say *'Julie, perhaps you are feeling anxious now and cannot bear waiting for me to come over. If you wait five minutes, do these five questions, I will be back'*.

(*For more strategies on ways to help pupils like Julie, see Chapter 3 and Chapter 4 on ambivalent-resistant attachment*).

Case Study (2) Mikey and his turmoil

Mikey is a 10-year-old pupil in year 6 of primary school. His teachers are all very worried about him. He exhibits worrying and erratic behaviour in school and at times seems totally unmanageable in lessons. He sometimes sits quietly doing his work and seems very engaged but is also very unpredictable. He often starts rocking in his chair and banging his head against the wall in the middle of classes, and continually runs out of lessons, sometimes hiding under the stairs and refusing to come out.

There appear to be no obvious triggers to these behaviours, which leave staff feeling helpless and concerned about his safety. He seems to have no real friends and is often in trouble for hitting other children in the playground. Other children find him annoying and at times frightening. Mikey has been offered specialist one-to-one counselling and behaviour support, but he finds it almost impossible to sit down quietly with a member of staff to discuss his behaviour. He often refuses to attend meetings, running in and out of the room, telling the support staff that he hates them all, that they are all rubbish at their jobs and that he does not have to do what they tell him.

There are, however, occasions when he appears to calm down, and he then shows that he is capable of age-appropriate work in some subjects. He is sometimes able to do this, for example in his Maths lessons, which he seems to enjoy. His teacher says, 'I always try to greet Mikey positively, even after a bad day, and I know it is better to praise Mikey quietly and privately for good work. I am really happy when he manages to complete a whole lesson, but there appears to be no real pattern to his behaviour. Sometimes, after a good lesson, he is impossible in my next lesson with him. It is very frustrating: you never know what mood he is going to be in.'

A space for reflection

- ⇨ What is your immediate reaction to this account of Mikey and his behaviour?
- ⇨ What extra information would you like to know?
- ⇨ What underlying defence mechanisms might be in operation?
- ⇨ What might be the attachment pattern?
- ⇨ What needs might Mikey be trying to fulfill?
- ⇨ How could his actions be re-framed with a positive intention?
- ⇨ What needs to happen to maintain a focus on learning and teaching?

Some extra information

Mikey has a fragmented and chaotic family history. His mother has given birth to seven children but only two of them live with her and her new partner. The other five live with their birth fathers and Mikey does not have contact with them, although he does remember them.

Mikey is the oldest child living at home and his mother has often told him that the only reason she has kept him was because his birth father did not want him. Mikey often comes into school tired, looking very dirty and unkempt. Social services and CAMHS (Child and Adolescent Mental Health Services) have been involved with the family for many years to varying degrees, but consistent contact with the family seems difficult.

There is a history of family non-attendance at meetings in school and with other support services. When Mikey's mother and his stepfather do attend meetings in school, they often express the desire for him to be taken away to 'boarding school' where he would be 'made to behave'. On other occasions, Mikey's mother gets upset in meetings and says she was sent away to a 'special school' and does not want it for Mikey.

A space for further reflection
- What do you think now?
- What pattern of behaviour does Mikey expect from adults?
- What are you now thinking about his anxieties, defences and attachment patterns?
- What are his needs, and what can the school building and adults in it offer Mikey?
- What emotional and mental state would it be important to maintain as his teacher?
- What strategies might work for Mikey?

What is happening for Mikey?

Mikey appears to be exhibiting an insecure/disorganised attachment pattern. He is erratic in his responses to adults and it is not always possible to see the immediate trigger for his extreme behaviour. Mikey has not had any experience of a secure base from which to explore the world: he has only experienced rejection and humiliation. He has not had any experience of being held in mind and thought about by a caring adult. This has led him to have little capacity for trust in relationships or thinking.

Mikey's basic need for safety and physical and emotional containment have scarcely been met. His brain has developed a response which is focused on survival. This means he is in a constant fight or flight mode, continually on high-alert for potential danger. He cannot trust positive relationships and praise from adults as he has had no experience of this. He quite simply has no space in his mind to think or engage in relationships. He appears to have developed the defence mechanisms of omnipotence (not allowing an adult to help or teach - see p.17) and spoiling (not able to have two consistently good lessons). He needs to rubbish the teacher and learning as he has been rubbished.

Mikey therefore needs school to provide a predictable structure with predictable reactions. It is important to remember that much of his difficult behaviour is prompted by overwhelming fear and anxiety. Teaching strategies need to focus on providing a strong, containing structure both for Mikey and for the staff who are dealing with him

If you were his teacher, you might be feeling helpless in the face of Mikey's behaviour. It is likely that these feelings are strong projections of the pupil's own helplessness and hopelessness. Make sure you have a strong support group and ask for regular meetings around the child. These meetings should not be called only in emergencies or as a reaction to an incident, but be set up as an on-going reflective process. In these meetings, all professionals need to be encouraged to name their feelings and anxieties, in order to acknowledge and manage the strain they are working under.

Mikey needs to know that there is a structure to school and learning which can withstand his painful feelings and enable him to feel SAFE.

PRACTICAL TEACHING STRATEGIES WHICH MIGHT HELP

- ✓ Use visual timetables if appropriate to show daily routines.

- ✓ Flag up any changes to routine in advance if possible, reflect back how catastrophic a change might feel. If there are going to be many changes in the day, for example the arrival of supply teachers, think about allowing this pupil to work somewhere safe with a trusted adult. If that is not possible, have a back-up plan in case they erupt in class or give them a timeout card to use. They may need, for example, to have a safe place to go to, where they can do simple worksheets and calm down.

- ✓ If possible, in class, allow them to sit near the teacher and near the door so that they can indicate if they need help and need to escape. Acknowledge how difficult it might be to stay in class and trust their ability to learn.

- ✓ Metaphor and creativity may be frightening. Make use of logical, left-brain, concrete tasks such as sorting, ordering, categorising, filling in and colouring in. These tasks will soothe their anxiety and provide some kind of logical order.

- ✓ These pupils quite literally need to be 'found' and brought back. Make use of activities which involve finding a missing link, putting something back into the picture, completing a puzzle, joining the dots, *Find Wally* books and so on.

- ✓ Take a small step-by-step approach. Find something they are good at and allow them to spend some time on this when they are out of other classes. This needs to be part of an agreed plan with key staff. It is not a 'reward' for bad behaviour, but an acknowledgement that they are still a capable person even when they have been unable to manage themselves in the classroom.

- ✓ For some pupils, such as Mikey, maths can be a 'safe container' as it involves clear right and wrong answers. Things can be taken apart and put back together.

(For more strategies on ways to help pupils like Mikey, see Chapter 3 and Chapter 4 on disorganised attachment)

Case Study (3) Paul's desire to control

Paul is in year 10 of secondary school and preparing for his GCSE exams. He is considered to be bright and capable of achieving high GCSE grades. However, he spends much of his time in the Head of Year's office or on temporary exclusions because of his aggressive behaviour, fighting and arguing with teachers.

His teachers have very divided opinions about him. Several teachers think that, despite his academic potential, his behaviour should not be tolerated and that he should be permanently excluded. They say he has no interest in anyone else except himself and he is a danger to other pupils. They also believe that it looks like he is getting special treatment because of his academic ability and this is not fair. Other teachers are very positive towards Paul, and think that he just needs some extra support and guidance. There have been several heated discussions in the staffroom about him.

He has recently been excluded from the technology workshops for health and safety reasons. In the last few weeks he had:

- *picked up a year 8 boy and held him upside down over the banisters until he cried*
- *been sent off in a key football match for arguing with the referee*
- *nearly had a fight with the Geography teacher and then told the teacher that he should have anger management classes because he was not fit to teach. This had led the teacher to get so angry that he told Paul he could 'take him on any time he wanted'*
- *not attended school for the past three days because he said he had been sent home and not told to come back, even though his Head of Year said he had not been excluded. Paul said he cannot come back until his 'exclusion' was discussed properly*
- *annoyed the Head of Science by not doing the work set in class, and insisting he should be given the revision books to do the work his own way at home*

A space for further reflection
⇨ What is your immediate reaction to this account of Paul and his behaviour?
⇨ What extra information would you like to know?
⇨ What underlying defence mechanisms might be in operation?
⇨ What might be the attachment pattern?
⇨ What needs might Paul be trying to fulfill?
⇨ How could this his action be re-framed with a positive intention?
⇨ What needs to happen to maintain a focus on learning and teaching?

Some extra information

It was known in this school by some of the key adults involved that Paul came from a family with a criminal background. His father had been shot when he was seven, and there had been a lot of negative publicity about him and a potential criminal connection. This had been reported in local and most national newspapers at the time. There had even been rumours that his mother had paid for the 'hit'.

After his father's death, his mother had begun drinking heavily, and was often not at home in the evenings. Paul was often at home alone and used to looking after himself. His mother rarely attended meetings at the school. When she did attend, she seemed distant and emotionally detached from Paul and his situation.

Paul rarely spoke about his home life. But he had told a teaching assistant that in primary school, he found reading difficult, and that his dad had spent a lot of time helping him improve.

A space for further reflection
- What do you think now?
- What pattern of behaviour does Paul expect from adults?
- What are you now thinking about his anxieties, defences and attachment patterns?
- What are his needs? How can these be met in the classroom and by the school?
- As his teacher, what emotional and mental state would it be important to maintain?
- What strategies might work for Paul?

What is happening for Paul?

It would seem that Paul is exhibiting omnipotence as a defence. It seems that his attachment pattern is fairly avoidant, and that he is keen to reject adults before they reject him. On the other hand, he can focus very effectively on an independent learning task, but wants staff to be available for him on his terms, as and when he wants them. His early experience of his father helping him to read suggests that he can accept adult help at times and this has probably helped him to progress in his learning.

He is also provoking a lot of staff into getting angry and rejecting him, something which is perhaps a familiar pattern for him, given that he may feel rejection and loss from his early years. Although he has had to take care of himself and act as an adult from an early age, in some ways he is still like a much younger child, not yet able to play by others' rules and unable to ask for help for fear of humiliation.

There is also a lot of splitting around Paul (see p.51). Staff are either very 'for' or 'against' keeping him in school, and he is the subject of endless discussions in the staffroom. He needs staff to be able to think about him in a containing way and for them to be consistent in how they address his needs. His desire for independent learning needs to be encouraged, not rejected. He may not be able to trust a relationship-based approach to teaching him, but can possibly be reached through mutual tasks and guidance on self-directed learning.

PRACTCAL STRATEGIES WHICH MIGHT HELP

Allow this pupil some control and choice over his activities where possible. This can often be built-in: e.g. 'There are two practice tasks, you can choose to do them in the order you think is best'.

- ✓ Tasks are the key. Work through a task to develop a relationship around it. Comment on the task when praising or providing feedback. For example, you might say: *'That's an interesting idea. I was wondering how old that boy in the story is?'* - rather than saying *'I'm really pleased with the ideas you've come up with, how about adding the age of the boy?'*.

- ✓ Notice the tasks he enjoys doing and can be fairly self-directed on. For example, allow him to have the Science revision books and ask him to show you the completed work when done.

- ✓ Organise group and project work - pupils like Paul sometimes prefer to work with peers and take on tasks which do not involve a direct relationship with the teacher.

- ✓ Design tasks which involve a product rather than a process: e.g. make a booklet, create a poster, write a newspaper article. Avoidant children like to see achievable goals. They can share their product without having to engage too much in the relationship.

- ✓ Use metaphor and story wherever possible. Activities where pupils such as Paul can draw, write or listen to stories, explore and discuss themes in books, on TV and film, use drama, objects or etc will be safer than those which ask them to speak directly about themselves.

- ✓ Work with other staff to ensure a consistent, positive approach which does not result in further rejecting Paul.

  (For more strategies on ways to help pupils like Paul, see Chapter 3 and Chapter 4 on avoidant attachment)

REFERENCES

Bion, W.R. (1962) A theory of thinking *International Journal of Psycho-Analysis, Vol 43* Reprinted in *Second Thoughts: Selected Papers on Psychoanalysis* (Maresfield Library)1984 London: Karnac Books

Bombèr, L. M. (2007) *Inside I'm Hurting: Practical strategies for supporting children with attachment difficulties in schools* London: Worth Publishing

Bowlby, J. (1988) *A Secure Base. Clinical Applications of Attachment Theory* London: Routledge

Covey, S. (1989) *The 7 Habits of Highly Effective People: Powerful lessons in personal change* New York: Simon & Schuster

Delaney, M. (2008) *Teaching the Unteachable* London: Worth Publishing

Delaney, M. (2010) *What Can I Do with the Kid Who … ?* London: Worth Publishing.

Delaney, M. (2016) *Into the Classroom: Special Educational Needs* Oxford: OUP

Dutton, J. & Heaphy, E. (2003) The Power of High Quality Connections In Carmeron, K., Duton, J. & Quinn, R. *Positive Organisational Scholarship* San Francisco, Barrett-Koehler

Galloway, D. (1985) *Schools, Pupils and Special Educational Needs* London: Croom Helm

Geddes, H. (2006) *Attachment in the Classroom: The links between children's early experience, emotional well-being and performance in school* London: Worth Publishing

Hanko, G. (1999) *Increasing Competence Through Collaborative Problem Solving* London: David Fulton

Layard, R. (2011) *Happiness: Lessons from a new Science* Second revised edition Penguin

McGonigal, K. (2015) *The Upside of Stress (Why stress is good for you and how to get good at it)* London: Vermilion

McDermot, I. & O'Connor, J. (2001) *Thorsons Way of NLP* London: Thorsons

Schofield, G. & Beek, M. (2006) *Attachment Handbook for Foster Care and Adoption* London: BAAF

Schore, A. N. (2001) The effects of a secure attachment relationship on right brain development, affect regulation and infant mental health *Infant Mental Health Journal* 22 p 7-66

Seligman, M. (2011) *Flourish: A new understanding of happiness and well-being* Nicholas Brealey Publishing

Sendak, M. (1963) *Where the Wild Things Are* UK: Red Fox

Taransaud, D. (2011) *You Think I'm Evil: Practical strategies for working with rebellious and aggressive adolescents* London: Worth Publishing

Terry, R., & Churches, R. (2007) *NLP for Teachers: How to be a highly effective teacher* New York: Crown House Publishing

Williams, M. & Penman, D. (2011) *Mindfulness: A practical guide to finding peace in a frantic world* London: Piatkus

Williams, S. (1994) *Managing Pressure for Peak Perfomance: The positive approach to stress* London: Kogan Page Ltd

Winnicott, D.W. (1971) *Playing and Reality* London: Routledge

TEDTALK Kelly McGonigal: How to make stress your friend TedTalk Ted Global June 2013

WEBSITES

Organisation	Website	
Adoption UK	adoptionuk.org	Resources and training for schools on teaching children who have been adopted
Caspari Foundation	caspari.org.uk	Training for staff in schools in Educational Psychotherapy principles and teaching children with attachment difficulties
Centre for Child Mental Health	childmentalhealthcentre.org	Training for staff on matters related to child mental health and attachment difficulties
Child Trauma Academy	childtrauma.org	Online trainings and information from Dr Bruce Perry on understanding and working with traumatised children
Dan Siegel	drdansiegel.com	Information and resources from the fields of neuroscience and attachment theory
Kids Are Worth It	kidsareworthit.com	Resources and articles by Barbara Coloroso on parenting and care giving of vulnerable children
Mindfulness in schools	mindfulnessinschools.org	Resources and ideas for implementing mindfulness in schools
Nurture group network	nurturegroups.org	Running nurture groups and using nurture principles in schools
Postadoption PAC-UK	pac-uk.org	Resources and training for schools on teaching children who have been adopted
The Learning Harbour	thelearningharbour.ie	**Information and training from Marie Delaney for education staff on teaching students with challenging behaviour and attachment difficulties**

Theraplay	theraplay.org.uk	A child and parent attachment model of training
The Yellow Kite attachment support service for schools	theyellowkite.co.uk	Information and training from Louise Bombèr and associates
Thrive	thethriveapproach.com	Resources and training on meeting the needs of children with attachment difficulties
National Archive	webarchive.national archives.gov.uk	Programmes for teaching children social, emotional skills (SEAL)
Winston's Wish	winstonswish.org.uk	Charity for bereaved children, has resources and advice on supporting bereaved children
Worth Publishing Ltd	worthpublishing.com	Books on all aspects of attachment, learning and behaviour for education professionals, parents and carers
Young Minds	youngminds.org.uk	Resources and information on promoting child and adolescent mental health

INDEX

Abuse 2, 27, 44,
Aggression 16, 45, 58, **62-4**, 86, 159
Anxiety 2, 6, 10, 18, 22, 30, **32-33**, 35, 36, 38, 45, 47, 48, 51, 61, 72-9, 82, 84, 85-6, 89, 92, 96, 102, 106, 112, 119, 126, 131, 132, 136, 137, 150, 151, 159, 164
Attachment *passim*:
Ambivalent-resistant, 21, 28, **32-37**, 55, 58, 59, 60, 62, 71, 102, 156, 169, 170: Avoidant, 21, **38-43**, 55, 58, 80, 106, 157, 177: Disorganised, 21, **44-51**, 54, 58, 59, 60, 62, 80, 159, 173-4
figure, 22-23, 55, **152**: insecure, 21, **27, 32-49**, 51, 55, 57, 107, 108, 169, 173: secure, 2, 20, 21, **22-26**, 50, 51, 55, 56, 60, 69, 108
Behaviour management 1, 2, 19
Classroom management 20, 25, **28-9**, 88, 93, *language for-*, 112-120
Communication 38, 68, 111, 114, 163, *difficulties with -*, 91, **106-109**
Containing *adult*, 11, 154, 177: *feelings*, 16, 36, **50**, 56, **79**, 104, 137: *school as a – structure*, 48, 50
Containment **22-3**, 36, **50**, 56, 75, 86, 102, 122, 152, 173; *maths as a -*, 174: *stories offering -*, 75
Control 10, 17, 18, 19, 38, 41, 42, 58, **74-5, 78-9**, 106, 123, 149, 150, **175-8**
Controlling 38, 44, 48, 151, 159
Defence 6, 38, 62, 70, 71, 74, 82, 83, 115, 168, 172, 176, 177: *mechanisms*, **11, 17, 51, 152, 155**, 161, 167, 171, 173, 175
Displacement 151, **152**
Empathy 24, 28, 45, 84, 90, **98-101**, 114, 132, 137, **138-9**, 160

Environment 2, 6, 17, 20, 25, 52, 60, 74, 76, 106, 116, 117, 123, 161: *creating a supportive -*, **28-30**
Fight or flight 31, 78, 92, 159, 173
Frustration 4, 23, 25, 33, 76, 81, 96, 102, 115, 151
Humiliation 23, 48, 58, 74, 80, 102, 117, 173, 177
Hypervigilance 58, **60-61**, 74, 75, 94, 159, 169
Independent 24, 26: *feels unable to be -*, 5, 32, 102: *wants to be -*, 38:
Language 61, 109: *inclusive -*, 71, 61: *pupil's -* 32, 107, 163: *teacher's choice of -*, 29, 31, 39, **111-129**
Learning Triangle 26, 32, 34, 40, 46, 55, 154
Loss 2, 27, 31, 74, 86, 88, 89, 90, 124, 133, 136, 137, 177
Manipulation 6, 36, 37, 58, **68-69**, 157
Mistakes 13, 25, 76, 77, 102, 103, 135, 145, 150, 151
Naming 22, 29, 33, 35, 39, 76, 77, 89, 101, 111, 115, **120-2**, 126, 132, 170, 171
Neglect 2, 44
Noticing 12-14, 16, 18, 29, 30, 31, 39, 41, 49, 51, 57, 67, 84, 89, 95, 97, 103, 107, 108, 111, **120-1**, 124-5, 126, 144, 145, 146, 148, 150, 156, 164, 178: *being noticed*, 42, 78;
Omnipotence 17, 18, 58, **74-75**, 159, 173, 177
Pattern 6, 18, 149, 155, 162: *of attachment*, 32, 38, 43, 44, 50, 56, 57, **58**, 60, 6203, 67, 71, 80, 84, 102, 106, 108, 156-9, 167-77: *of behaviour*, **14**, 16, 19, 27, 36-7, 41, 42, 45, 48, 55, 57, 115, 147

Pause for thought 12, 16, 18, 20, 37, 43, 49, 108, 126, 142, 143, 145
Perfectionism 12-13, 58, **76-7**, 151
Problem-solving 33, 92, 136, **139**
Projection **10-12**, 81, 149, 139, 173
Risk *of exclusion*, 2: *factors*, 27: *at -*, 44: *taking - in learning*, 25, 38, 76, 102, 135, 158: *no - activity*, 31
Safe 2, 40, 41, 46, 75, 78, 79, 99, 111, 116, 135, 136, 139, 168 *boundaries*, 17: *class*, 3, 20, 26, 101, 112, 117: *environment*, 25, 76, 161: *feeling -*, 15, 25, 28, 30, 48, 53, 60, 62, 72: *place* 47, 174: *school as a safe haven*, 2, 50
Safety 20, 21, 22, **27**, 28, 45, **48**, 53, 56, 60, 61, 74, 78, 89, 114, **117**, 127, 132, 152, 171, 173, 175
Secure base 55, 169, 173
Self-esteem 66, 73, 91, **102-5**
Splitting *as psychological defence*, 49, **51**, 68, 70, 177: *in maths*, 136: *- up*, 86:
Strain zone 142, 147, 148
Stress *hormone*, 92: *pupil*, 16, 21, 27, 31, 61, 82, 83, 89, 148: *related illness*, 50: *teacher -*, 4, 13, 19, 115, 141, **142-144**, 145, 147, 149, 153:
Transference 15, 62, 115
Transitions 47, **85-88**
Trauma 2, 27, 74, 82, 83, 90, 92, 124, 132
Turn-taking 16, 23, 25, 29, 52, 53, 54, 98, 100, **103**, 120
Violence *domestic -*, 27, 44, 152: *re-creating -*, 58, **62-65**
Wellbeing 9-10, **141-153**
Wondering 12, 35, 59, 77, 178: *aloud*, 18, 112, **125**, 126, 128, 162
Working memory 82, 91, **92-97**